The *ART* *of*
TEACHING
CHILDREN

The ART of TEACHING CHILDREN

BY
DARYL V. HOOLE
Donette V. Ockey

ILLUSTRATIONS
DICK AND MARY SCOPES

Published By
DESERET BOOK COMPANY
Salt Lake City, Utah
1972

Second Edition
Revised and Enlarged
1972
ISBN No. 87747-455-9

Printed by

DESERET NEWS PRESS

in the United States of America

DEDICATION

To our parents, Donovan H. and
Ada S. Van Dam, who exemplify
the message of this book.

ACKNOWLEDGMENTS

The preparation of this material has been aided by the suggestions and contributions of our mother, Mrs. Donovan H. Van Dam. We appreciate our many friends who have shared with us choice thoughts and ideas, especially Mrs. Douglas D. Alder and Mrs. Ronald D. Banks. We are particularly grateful for the cooperation and help of our husbands, H. J. M. Hoole, Jr. and Gail W. Ockey, in making this book possible.

CONTENTS

INTRODUCTION

Every child has a right to be
Well bred
Well fed
Well led

"BOY LOST—Forest rangers, volunteers, helicopter service unfaltering in their search to find boy lost in mountain area."

Headlines, such as the one quoted above, appear frequently in newspapers. With each incident, heroic efforts are put forth by searching parties—often at the peril of the individuals' own lives—to find the lost one. Countless examples could be cited regarding the heroism extended for the physical well-being of another person. No effort is too great to save a life.

As parents, the physical well-being of our children is constantly in our thoughts. We wouldn't even consider letting our children toy with danger; we wouldn't think of sending them out in cold weather without adequate clothing; we work diligently so that their bodies are well fed. We, as good parents, do everything possible for our children's physical welfare. If we should become negligent in our responsibilities, law enforcement officers could take away our children.

The pages to follow are dedicated to the spiritual welfare of our children. If we are negligent in our responsibilities here, we will lose our children—this time forever.

The Lord has said, "For behold, this is my work and my glory—to bring to pass the immortality and eternal life of man." (Pearl of Great Price, Moses 1:39.)

Our Father in heaven has given to parents the responsibility of working with him in this task of saving souls. He has told us that if we do not teach our children, the sin will be upon our heads.

In the book, *Home, the Savior of Civilization,* McCulloch says:

Of all the factors that enter into the environment of a child, or of anyone else for that matter, the home is by far the most powerful, so much so, that one may say that home either makes or mars character. The child from the day of his birth, for at least twelve years, is so dominated by the influences of the home, whether good or evil, that he is absolutely helpless to resist them.

A noted psychologist has said that he could take any five babies at birth, and by placing them in certain environments (homes) he could make of each of them a hobo, a thief, a murderer, a doctor, or a lawyer.

This is a debatable statement, but it does point out the importance the home environment plays in the development of a child. A person's chances for failure or success in life are greatly influenced by his surroundings.

The Lord has given us precious children and has asked us to provide for them the best home we are capable of, that they might have the opportunity of developing their personal qualities to the fullest extent. Our children are choice spirits; the responsibility of bringing them up as the Lord would desire is the greatest calling and challenge of our lives.

In a communication from the First Presidency of The Church of Jesus Christ of Latter-day Saints to the Church Correlation Committee, published in the *Improvement Era,* December 1962, this statement was given: "The home is the basis of a righteous life, and

no other instrumentality can take its place nor fulfil its essential functions."

A fifteen-year-old girl eloped. Her parents took
steps to have the marriage annulled but learned that
their daughter was going to have a baby. In bitterness
the father said, "This shows how little value there is
to church teaching. She has gone to church all her life."

Actually, of the one hundred sixty-eight hours a
week, a child's church instruction averages only four
hours at the most. A child's week can be divided somewhat as follows:

        38 hours at school
         4 hours at church
        70 hours sleeping
        ____
       112 total

       168 total hours in a week
      —112
      ____
        56 hours in the home environment

This gives parents an average of eight hours a day
when their children are directly under their influence
and supervision. These hours total more than the com-
bined hours of both school and church. A child's destiny
is largely determined by what parents do with this
time.

The early imprint of home and family life is never
erased. It might become blurred, smeared, and
smudged, but it is never erased and forgotten.

A young mother said:

Being a mother is an opportunity which will come to me
only once. Unlike a beautiful oil painting which an artist

labors over for a long period of time, I will not be able to
retouch the finished product. My work as a mother must be
done each day to the best of my ability, for as I contemplate
the finished fruits of my labor in years to come, the attitudes
I have transmitted, the examples I have set, the memories I
have sealed, the lessons I have taught, and the values I have
helped form will not be able to be recalled, undone, or painted
over.

> I took a piece of plastic clay
>   And idly fashioned it one day,
> And as my fingers pressed it still,
>   It moved and yielded to my will.
>
> I came again when days were past—
>   The bit of clay was hard at last;
> The form I gave it, it still bore,
>   But I could change that form no more.
>
> I took a piece of living clay
>   And gently formed it day by day,
> And molded with my power and art
>   A young child's soft and yielding heart.
>
> I came again when years were gone—
>   It was a man I looked upon;
> He still that early impress wore,
>   And I could change him nevermore.
>
> (Author unknown.)

Every day a parent should ask himself: "Have I
taught my child a gospel truth today? Have I done
something, either through word or example, to help
my child see, hear, or feel something which will build
his understanding and develop a noble character? Do
gospel teachings and standards make up the atmosphere of our home? Am I alert to every opportunity to
teach a child a lesson? If enough opportunities do not
present themselves, do I create such an opportunity
or do I set the stage so a lesson can be learned? Do I
realize that the gospel comprises not only scriptures

and doctrine, but also that it is the way of life, that it represents true values? Have I taught my child a gospel truth today?"

We probably won't be able to teach our children everything there is to know about the gospel, but it is up to us as parents to lay the foundation and prepare them to be receptive to all worthy teachings throughout their lives. The Church auxiliary organizations are limited and cannot give children a total understanding of the gospel, but the children who have had gospel training in their homes are better able to understand and appreciate lessons taught them in Sunday School, Primary, MIA, and seminary; for example, a three-year old child was taught the basic concept of counting from one to ten, and now she can frequently be heard to say, "eleven, twelve, thirteen. . . ." But until she was taught the fundamentals she was not able to comprehend numbers at all.

The true purpose of teaching by parents is to prepare children to stand on their own two feet, to become mature, responsible, useful people. *Home is the training ground for life.*

One important goal of life is to learn to master oneself. First, a parent must achieve this, and then he will be prepared to guide children in doing likewise.

As parents, we are to help each of our children develop according to his own potential, not that of his father or sister. We should help children overcome weaknesses and poor personality traits, but we must not expect them to be talented and gifted in just the same way their older brother may be. *Help your child become the best of whatever he is.*

A young boy who was shorter in stature than average was pitied by his parents. They made him understand that because he was so small, not much was expected of him, and he just couldn't compete with other boys his age. His size was used as an excuse in everything he did.

Another young boy who was very short for his age was told by his parents that he would have to prove to the world that he was a man. He has done that very thing and is a giant in character and spirituality, though he is small physically.

A secret formula for handling children is: "Treat the child as if he were as you want him to be, and he will usually respond accordingly." A person tends to become what you think he is. Let your children sense your value of them and your hopes and expectations for them. Build them up rather than tear them down. When you see them doing the things you want them to do, compliment them. Sincere commendation and praise will encourage them to be good.

The former Utah Senator, Arthur V. Watkins, tells that after attending Brigham Young University he started teaching fourth and fifth grades in the Maeser Elementary School. He was told that his salary would be $40 a month. Mr. Watkins asked how much sheepherders were paid. One of the school trustees, a sheep rancher, replied that the herders were paid $60 a month, because they were responsible for valuable property. Mr. Watkins responded: "I won't work for less than the sheepherders; children are a lot more valuable than sheep." He was paid $60 a month.

A group of men were contemplating building a million dollar gymnasium for boys. Someone asked, "Isn't that price high?"

Horace Mann responded: "Not if it is my boy."

A missionary who had served three years in Ireland gave a farewell talk at the conclusion of his mission before leaving for home. It went something like this: "Brothers and sisters, I think my mission has been a failure. I have labored all my days here as a missionary and have baptized only one dirty little Irish kid. That's all I have done."

This man then returned to his home somewhere in Montana. Years later a gentleman went to visit him. He said to the missionary, "Do you remember that you said you thought your mission was a failure because you had baptized only one dirty little Irish kid?"

"Yes, I do remember that," the man replied.

"Well, I would like to shake your hand. My name is Charles A. Callis of the Council of the Twelve of The Church of Jesus Christ of Latter-day Saints. I am that dirty little Irish kid you baptized on your mission."

You don't know who the little boy in your family really is! He may be the future bishop of a ward, the future mayor of a city, the future governor of a state, or the doctor into whose hands lives are committed, or the church leader who will be the prophet, seer, and revelator of our Father in heaven.

Be patient with your little boy (or girl) and teach him the gospel. He is the man of tomorrow. He is a child of God.

A Sunday School teacher came to her superintendent one Sunday morning and with discouragement in her voice and on her face said, "I am not teaching this morning."

He asked, "Why?"

She answered, "I have only one boy today."

Quickly he told her to believe in that one boy. For all he knew there was another Cromwell to dissolve a Parliament or another Beethoven to touch the world's heart strings. Rather reluctantly she went back to that one boy.

"I have only one boy today." Her words set me to thinking. The superintendent recalled that somebody has said that history is filled with instances where one vote, just one, has decided elections of tremendous importance. Was it not by one vote that Aaron Burr missed being President of the United States? Was it not one vote that made California a part of the Union and thus turned the tide of immigration westward? Was it not one vote that elected Oliver Cromwell to the famous "Long Parliament," sent Charles I to the scaffold and set Great Britain free? Was it not one vote in the electoral college in 1876 that decided who should be the President of the United States?

"I have only one boy today!" Yet he remembered that no learned society discovered America, but one man—Columbus. And no Parliament saved English liberties, but one man —Coke, and no confederate nations rescued Scotland from her political and ecclesiastical enemies, but one man—John Knox. In the spring of 1820 it wasn't a group of learned men who went into a grove to seek God, but one boy—Joseph Smith. And the disgraceful nursing system was reformed not by co-operative clubs of interested women, but one woman—Florence Nightingale.

"I have only one boy today!" Only one, and yet he matters just as much as the figure *one* matters on a clock or watch. He matters just as much as the figure *one* on the multiplication table; just as much as the letter A in the alphabet, just as much as *one* man matters to the woman at the wedding hour, and just as *one* woman matters to the groom on his wedding day. Someone has taught that *one* may be many. Andrew brought Simon Peter—just one man, but that one was also many, for Peter brought 3,000 to God in one sermon in one day.

"I have only one boy today!" What of him? Win him. He may be many!

(Author unknown.)

There are many areas through which a parent might work to lead effectively and guide a child so that he might live a happy, worthy life, enabling him to return to the presence of his Father in heaven. We will discuss nine areas. Each of these areas is like a piece of a picture puzzle. If one should be neglected, there would be a blank spot in the life of your child.

His picture would be incomplete. If you as a parent strive to include all nine areas as you influence and train a child, they would form a complete, ideal picture of the way of life which can lead to eternal life and joy forever and ever.

EXAMPLE

PUZZLE PIECE I

"There are only three ways to teach a child. The first is by example. The second is by example. The third is by example."
—Albert Schweitzer

Children make use of whatever is before them. A schoolteacher noticed that one little boy was drawing everything in black crayon. He drew black horses, black cows, and black cars. The teacher was disturbed about this morbid, negative tendency in the boy and called a meeting of the little boy's parents, the principal of the school and a psychiatrist. The psychiatrist found out that the reason the boy used a black crayon to color everything was because a black crayon was the only crayon he had.

With what does your child have to work?

Children Learn What They Live

If a child lives with criticism, he learns to condemn,
If a child lives with hostility, he learns to fight
If a child lives with fear, he learns to be apprehensive
If a child lives with pity, he learns to feel sorry for himself.
If a child lives with ridicule, he learns to be shy.
If a child lives with jealousy, he learns to be envious.
If a child lives with shame, he learns to feel guilty,
If a child lives with encouragement, he learns to be confident.
If a child lives with tolerance, he learns to be patient.
If a child lives with praise, he learns to be appreciative.
If a child lives with acceptance, he learns to love.
If a child lives with approval, he learns to like himself.
If a child lives with recognition, he learns that it is good to
have a goal.
If a child lives with sharing, he learns about generosity.
If a child lives with honesty and fairness, he learns what truth
and justice are.
If a child lives with security, he learns to have faith in himself and those about him.
If a child lives with friendliness, he learns that the world is a
nice place in which to live.
If YOU live with serenity, your child will live with peace of
mind.

—Dorothy Law Nolte

Confucius asked: "How can mother crab teach young son to walk straight forward, when she herself walks sideways?"

We as parents must be certain that the example set for our children is the correct one.

A surveyor walking around an army post on the edge of a western town became acquainted with the soldier who fired the cannon for retreat each evening. "Do you fire this cannon at the same time each evening?" he asked.

"Yes," the soldier replied. "At six o'clock on the dot, and I time it carefully with this watch. I check it every day by the jeweler's clock, two blocks from here."

Several days later the surveyor entered the jeweler's shop and engaged the jeweler in conversation. "That's a mighty fine looking clock you have there," indicating the prominent timepiece in the window.

"Yes, it's a good clock; it keeps perfect time," answered the jeweler. "In fact, that clock hasn't varied a second in two years."

"That's really marvelous," exclaimed the surveyor.

"True, and we have a perfect check on it, too," elaborated the jeweler. "Every evening at exactly six o'clock they fire a cannon over at the fort, and this clock is always right on the dot!"

(Author unknown.)

One day several small children were overheard as they were playing house. Roger was the daddy and was preparing to leave for priesthood meeting. Jean commented that it was Sunday and she wasn't going to clean her house. A few minutes later she pretended she was giving a lesson in Relief Society. Then later they played Sunday School and sang the little hymns they had learned there.

It's certain that if Daddy frequented the local pool hall or if Mother spent her time at bridge parties or devoted the Sabbath day to housework, the children would have picked that up and played that type of part instead.

One evening as he was bathing, a husband ordered his wife to bring him a towel. The next evening his young daughter was in the tub and asked for a towel, using his exact demanding words and tone of voice. It was then that the father was struck with the significance of setting the right example.

One day as Jean was playing house, she was heard to say, "I'm going to wipe this bottle off before I put it in my refrigerator like Mother does, and then my refrigerator will stay nice and clean." She had never been told anything about this; she learned it through observation.

A mother can tell just what kind of mother she is by watching her little girls play with their dolls!

"A boy does not have to be shown a mark on the wall to measure up to when there is a man around about the size he wants to be."

An army officer was instructing his troops prior to a battle and said, "Men! Here is your ammunition. Fight until it is gone and then run." Then he added, "I'm a little lame, so I'm going to start running now."

Some parents, like this army officer, believe that there is a double standard. They honestly feel that what applies to their children doesn't necessarily apply to them. They really believe that they live in a different world—one for their children and one for them.

We wouldn't think of teaching our children to lie, but it is an all too common practice for a young child to answer the door by saying, "Mommie says to tell you she's not home."

An MIA teacher had inspired a group of girls through her beautiful lessons on modesty and chastity. A few months later some of these same girls observed this former teacher standing in her daughter's wedding reception line wearing a dress which defied all she had been talking about. Her beautiful words were forgotten in an instant; only the lesson of what she did remained in the minds of the young girls.

These young girls would be inclined to agree with the boy who said: "What Dad said is a good idea, but nobody does it, not even Dad!"

Ed Nicholson is a buyer in a large department store. Ed is past forty, tall, grayhaired—the kind of man you would call "distinguished." And, in his way, Ed is distinguished.

He is an officer in the Parent-Teacher Association. He is vice-chairman of his civic group, and he likes to read "good" books. Once, his friends talked of nominating him for councilman on a local reform ticket.

A few weeks ago, Ed came home and set a large package down on the dining-room table. His wife couldn't help noticing how his eyes shone as he gazed at it.

"What's in it, dear?" she asked.

"Wait till you see!" he exulted.

He tore off the wrappings and revealed a handsome mantel clock, set in the rich mahogany of a ship's wheel. "Ed," his wife breathed, "it's lovely. But it must have cost a fortune. Can we afford it?"

"We certainly can. It didn't cost us a cent. I took it from the stockroom. It's got a scratch somewhere on the base and it has been lying around for months. So we might as well put it to good use."

Nicholson virtually glowed with pride over his achievement.

"Golly, Dad," said twelve-year-old Tommy, "that was clever. It's sure a keen clock."

"The word is 'surely,'" Nicholson corrected him. "But it IS keen."

To his son, Tommy, Ed was saying, as though he spoke the words: "There's nothing wrong with my taking this clock; nothing wrong with taking stamps home from the office; nothing wrong with cheating on your income tax."

Maybe Tommy won't ever reach into his mother's purse for a quarter to go to the movies; maybe he won't climb a fence and steal a ripe watermelon; maybe he won't swipe a toy from the Five and Ten. But if he does any of these things, his course will have been charted. He will have had an example set for him right in his home.

—Peter Nelson
"Let's Take Off Our Moral Blinders"
Coronet Magazine
August 1951

Our children must never be able to say, "We couldn't hear what you said because your actions were ringing so loudly in our ears." We must live the way we teach. Our every act must be a sermon to our children. Melvin J. Ballard said, "The greatest sermon any of us will ever preach will be the sermon of our lives."

The Savior set the pattern when he said, "Come, follow me. . . ."

In Palestine, visitors are impressed when they notice that there the shepherd walks *ahead* of his flock.

As parents we are busy with the cares of supporting and caring for a family, and sometimes we don't have all the time we would like to teach our children. But teaching through example requires no time. It takes no longer to be a good example than to be a poor one.

Another attribute of example is that we don't influence just one, but many.

A stranger was traveling through a dense London fog and was unable to find his way back to his hotel. He met a young lad and said, "Show me the way back to my hotel and I'll give you a shilling."

The young boy replied, "Follow me and my light, sir. I know my way well."

Following the steady beam of the boy's light, they walked single file to the hotel.

"Thank you," said the traveler, "here is your coin. You've earned it."

"And here is my coin," said the second voice from the darkness.

"Here is mine, too," said a third person. "I saw your light and believed you knew where you were going."

"Thanks," said the boy. "I surely didn't know I was leading so many."

Down the aisle of life walk those who reflect you. How will they be?

"THE MOTHER MAKES US MOST"

PUZZLE PIECE II

"Mothers sow the seeds in childhood that determine to a great extent life's harvest in adulthood."
—President David O. McKay

Mother reigns as a queen, remaining serene
    Midst confusion, bedlam, and noise;
An ingenious spender, a fantastic mender
    Of clothes, children, and toys.

She can turn something tragic, almost by magic
    Into something that's really quite slight;
She can get up at dawn, weed the yard, mow the lawn
    And still stay up half the night.

She's quite a mechanic and when things get frantic
    She always has a solution;
When her son's been a brute, she can smooth the dispute
    Without causing a small revolution.

She finds money for braces in impossible places
  And knows how to tackle a budget;
She wants her home nice, yet she'll sure sacrifice
  And never even begrudge it.

And when there's confusement, provides instant amusement
  For children who need her attention;
Wipes up dozens of spills, pays all sorts of bills
  For things too numerous to mention.

She combines patterns and laces, brings smiles to girls' faces
  By creating a dream of a dress;
Most days she is harried with chores many and varied,
  Yet somehow she's found happiness.

Or perhaps a mother is defined just as well in this essay written by an eight-year-old and titled "What a Mom Means to a Kid:"

> A mother is a person who takes care of her kids and gets their meals and if she's not there when you get home from school, you wouldn't know how to get your dinner and you wouldn't feel like eating it anyhow.

President David O. McKay said: "If I were asked to name the world's greatest need, I should say unhesitatingly, wise mothers."

A mother's influence is one of the greatest influences, for either good or evil, in the world. Her influence actually begins before a child is born when her health habits, activities, and diet play a part in forming the little body within her.

As a mother bathes her newborn child and keeps it sweet and warm and lovable in soft, clean clothing, she is establishing a pattern of habits which will influence the child's future physical health. A few years later cleanliness becomes an essential qualification to the child for little friends and playmates. We observe that our children, without any bidding from us, seek out other children for friends who are clean and well cared for. A mother soon discovers how naturally the teachings of cleanliness of body can be directed to the teaching of cleanliness of the mind. Rumford said: "So great is the effect of cleanliness upon man that it extends to his moral character."

Cleanliness in the home is also definitely connected with cleanliness of body and mind. Neither unsanitary conditions nor neglect breed good physical or mental health. Actually, good health is a product of cleanliness. The mother plays the major role here.

Order in the home is conducive to order of mind, and order of mind sets the stage for success and accomplishment. Of course the mother is the stage manager and directs the order of the home.

President J. Reuben Clark, Jr., summed up the purpose behind cleanliness and order and mental and physical health when he said: "A healthy body plus a healthy mind is the very best nursery for a healthy spirit."

A baby is a bundle of possibilities. He isn't a human being. He is a human becoming. As he becomes someone, the mother under normal conditions exerts the greatest influence.

In fact, Tennyson tells us: "The Mother Makes Us Most."

Not only does a mother play the leading part in influencing the physical welfare of her children, but her effect on their spiritual and emotional development is paramount in their lives. President McKay has said: "Mothers sow the seeds in childhood that determine to a great extent life's harvests in adulthood." Then he carried this further when he quoted:

Sow a thought, reap an act,
Sow an act, reap a habit,
Sow a habit, reap a character,
Sow a character, reap an eternal destiny.
                              (Author unknown)

A mother must have the patience, the persever-
ance, and the know-how to bring a tiny baby to a full
expression of its talents and capabilities. Again her
influence reaches back to the prenatal period when her
wholesome attitude helps a little spirit to know that it
is wanted. A mother's love, demonstrated through the
warmth and closeness of her body, and her feelings
reflected in her tone of voice are as vital to the growth
and development of a baby as are food and warmth. Her
understanding of him and appreciation for him are
like sunshine to his soul.

"There are helpful books on child guidance and
helpful rules to follow," says Mrs. Klea Worsley, coun-
seling psychologist at Brigham Young University, "but
even if you haven't read the books and don't know all
the rules—even if you make every blunder—your children will probably come through it all right if *you love
them and they feel that love.*" Mrs. Worsley says two
of the most important keys to handling children are to
love and to *listen.*

Although it is possible to indulge and over-protect
children, it is impossible to give them too much *love.*
A child should feel loved at all times. Even when it is
necessary to reprimand or punish a child, he should
understand you do it out of love for him and that you
are in no way rejecting him. Remember, children need
love most when they deserve it least! Love involves
many things including a great deal of patience and
understanding. Mothers should consciously work to
develop these traits as they rear their families.

one free. Obedience must not be blind. Don't make your children mind you just to please you. Help them to learn obedience because it is the right thing to do— the way of joy and success. Help your children understand *why* they must obey. The Prophet Joseph Smith gave us the inspired formula for achieving this when he said, "Teach people correct principles and then they can govern themselves." For some practical helps in accomplishing this with children, please refer to page 228.

A mother must teach her children discipline. She must understand that the word "discipline" is a derivation of "disciple" which means "to follow." Discipline is not just a series of punishments, but it is a pattern for teaching and instruction. The dictionary says that it is the training which corrects, molds, strengthens, or perfects.

Discipline should be kind and loving, yet firm; never harsh. When the Beehive House in Salt Lake City was restored, an unusual built-in pipe-like device was discovered in the house. Investigation revealed that this was a Pioneer-style inter-com system designed by Brigham Young to aid mothers in calling their children. Brigham Young said, "A mother is never at her best when yelling at her children."

First, a child must learn discipline of body. A body is the temple of God and must be kept clean and pure and holy. A child must learn discipline of mind. We become what we think. A person's true character is revealed by what he thinks about when he doesn't have to think. A worthy mother will help condition her children's thinking towards wholesome, uplifting thoughts. A healthy body and a healthy mind produce a healthy spirit, and a healthy spirit leads to exaltation in the kingdom of God.

A mother implants in the hearts of her children the values which will be highly significant in determining their destiny. A value is that which has priority in the life of a person, that which he prizes. True values represent the best judgment of man in tune with the mind and will of the Lord. Following are some of the values a mother's influence helps form:

Oneself—Your children will feel as important as you make them feel. Through you they can find confidence and courage. You can instil within them the quest to excel. It has been said, "If you think you can or can't, you are right." A mother teaches her children that they can. Dorothy Canfield Fisher said, "A mother is not a person to lean on, but a person to make leaning unnecessary." You can teach them that they are children of God and have divine attributes and gifts which are to be developed for their progress and ultimate perfection.

Attitudes—Your children will tend to look at life the way you do. A healthy attitude is more important than mental ability in the well-being and success of a person.

Habits—Your children will tend to do things the way you do. Habits become the iron bands of character and personality.

Time—Your children will tend to place as much value on time as you do. A person succeeds and progresses in life in direct proportion to the way he uses his time. His eternal destiny is also determined by his use of time because it is impossible to kill time without injuring eternity.

Industry—Your children will tend to apply themselves to a task just as you do. They will reflect your enthusiasm and ambition, your zest for living. "Nothing great was ever wrought without enthusiasm."

Work—Your children will consider work either a blessing or a burden, just as you do.

Language—Your children will tend to express themselves as you do, with regard to proper grammar and to the wise selection of words. Our choice of words and manner of expression reveal all that we are.

Morals—Your children will tend to hold sacred that which you treasure. A person is as strong as his morals. A mother doesn't teach morals from a long list of do's and don't's. Her teaching must reach out from her heart and touch the hearts of her children, so that they become so emotionally involved with righteousness that every fibre of their being is in tune with moral purity.

Money—Your children will tend to regard money in the same light you do. To them it will be the end in itself or the means to an end, just as it is with you. They will be just as generous with their means as you are.

Graciousness—Your children will likely follow your example here. From you they can learn to say or do the right thing, in the nicest way, at the right time.

Thoughtfulness—Through you your children will learn to do unto others as they would be done by.

Gratitude—Your children will tend to feel and express appreciation just as you do. Teach them that the greatest of all virtues is a thankful heart.

Service—Through your example, your children will learn that the greatest joy in life lies in service to others. Someone said, "Service is the rent we pay for the space we occupy on earth." By serving our fellow men we serve the Lord, because he has said, "Inasmuch as ye have done it unto one of the least of these my brethren, ye have done it unto me."

Homemaking—Your daughters will reflect your attitude and your skills in this greatest of all callings. Help them to feel through you that homemaking is a divine appointment; a creative calling; the noblest, most rewarding work a woman can do. Prepare them for this calling by teaching them homemaking skills and successful management. Encourage your daughters to study and develop themselves in all areas, because the greater their knowledge and abilities, the more effective their homemaking can be, and the richer their lives and those of their children can be.

Religion—Your children will tend to feel just as you do about the gospel. You can help them to make it the greatest thing in their lives.

The only real way a mother can teach these values is by offering a model for identification. Values are caught, not taught. Values are gained through "value-ing." The way to determine whether or not a stick is crooked is to lay it alongside a straight one.

A noted educator stated: "The education of the soul for eternity should begin and be carried on at the fireside." The years for influencing the life of a child are fleeting. A mother must use them well or they will quickly pass her by.

Have You Seen Them

Have you seen, anywhere, a tall little lad
And a wee winsome lass of four?
'Twas only today, barefooted and brown,
That they played by my kitchen door.
'Twas only today—or maybe a year?
It couldn't be twenty, I know,
They were calling for me to help in their game
But I was too busy to go.
Too busy with sweeping and dusting to play
And now they have silently wandered away.

If perchance you hear of this slim little lad
And this wee winsome lass of four,
I pray you tell me.
To find them again I would journey this wide world o'er.
Somewhere, I'm sure, they'll be playing a game,
And should they be calling for me
To come out and help them,
Oh, tell them, I beg, I'm coming as fast as can be!
For there's never a house might hold me today
Could I hear them call me to join in their play.

Minnie Case Hopkins

Even mothers who consider themselves too busy to play with their children or to enjoy creative activities with them or to read to them and teach them would be able to find the time to do so if they would organize their lives, get their work down to a system, and learn to use their time well and teach their children to help in the home. When planning and scheduling the activities of the day, include time for your children. You will never find the time unless you plan for it, work for it and then *take the time.* (For suggestions regarding scheduling and systematizing, refer to *The Art of Homemaking* by Daryl V. Hoole, Salt Lake City: Deseret Book Company, 1963.)

It is good for both your children and you to have them assist you with housework so there will be time for creative fun, stories, and other activities which help a child develop to his potential. (For specific suggestions and helps, please refer to "How to Do Less for Your Children So You Can Do More with Them" on page 221.) A mother of ten children has things so well organized that the work gets done and she has time for each child as well as for herself. Every child is assigned certain tasks, and each older child is in charge of helping a younger child dress and carry out his chores. This team begins working early on a summer's morning and by ten o'clock the routine work is done. The rest of the day is devoted to cooking, creative activities, lessons and classes, picnics, visits to museums and other places of interest, short trips, and many other ventures which lend such richness to their lives.

Mothers must learn to use their minutes to the fullest extent. While dressing and changing a baby, talk to him, sing to him, and laugh and play with him. While ironing, cooking, washing dishes, or sewing, a mother can call her children around her and talk with them, tell them stories, teach them, and enjoy their companionship.

A mother's motto could well be: *"Be where you are."* Instead of being preoccupied with the cares of the day, a mother should be alert to every opportunity to enjoy and influence her children.

She is available and eager to visit with children as they return home from school. The confidence and companionship built up in this manner are priceless.

A Cookie and a Kiss

A house should have a cookie jar
For when it's half past three
And children hurry home from school
As hungry as can be,
There's nothing quite so splendid
In filling children up
As spicy, fluffy ginger cakes
And sweet milk in a cup.

A house should have a mother
Waiting with a hug
No matter what the boy brings home—
A puppy or a bug,
For children only loiter
When the bells ring to dismiss,
If no one's home to greet them
With a cookie and a kiss.

Author Unknown

Teenagers are greatly blessed when they can return home from a date or party and discuss freely their activities with their parents. In the early days of childhood the habit of talking things over should be cultivated. Then even during the teen years the lines of communication will be open.

Set aside a special time, both daily and weekly, to teach children. (Spontaneous occasions are valuable, too!) In addition to our weekly family night, we enjoy a "story hour" each evening. After the toys are picked up and the children are ready for bed, we spend time singing, saying the alphabet, counting, reciting poems, and reading stories. This is as routine as putting on the pajamas. (The singing and counting can actually begin during the picking up and undressing processes. This makes bed preparations go more smoothly and creates a happy attitude in the minds of the children about going to bed.) In addition to the stories and singing, we have a simple, yet meaningful routine which has become the highlight of our children's lives. The children and I recall the activities of the day and then each child tells what his or her "Happiest Experience" has been. We talk about these happy experiences for a minute and discuss how we would like to enjoy them again sometime. Then we talk for just a minute about any little problems that may have occurred and encourage the children to try to improve in that particular regard and to avoid such mistakes again. Then we kneel for prayers, and as each child prays, instead of speaking in generalities or mimicking someone else, he expresses thanks for his happy experience and asks the Lord to help him to do better with regard to a problem or act of disobedience.

Frequently during the day one of our children will say, "Oh, Mommy, I'm going to make this be my

happiest experience for today." Or one of them will
exclaim, "This has been such a happy day. I wonder
what my very happiest experience will be!"

We feel that our "Happiest Experience" time each
evening can be a character-building routine and will
help our children form the habit of looking for the best
in life and trying to grow and improve each day.

Then as I tuck our children in bed and give them
one last kiss I say to them, "What is my wish for
you?" They usually express the deep feelings of a
parent's heart by responding, "To be a good boy and
always try to do what is right." Then I take just a
few minutes by each bedside to spend some time alone
with each child. I visit about several pleasant matters. (At this hour children are usually eager to pro-
long bed time as long as possible, so I find that they
are eager to confide in me and tell me things which perhaps they didn't take time for in their busy day.) Also,
they will listen with rapt attention to anything a parent has to say. Our children love this intimate time
alone and won't go to sleep without their visit. This
"visit" sets the mood for sweet dreams and helps build
beautiful philosophies in the minds of children.

Although this routine sounds somewhat involved,
it is easily established and doesn't take much time.
For instance, "What is my wish for you" takes only a
few seconds as does the "Happiest Experience." Of
course, such a routine can be adapted to any situation,
and perhaps in very large families you could visit with
half the children one night and the other half the next.
No matter how you decide to do it, you will derive ever-
lasting dividends from this traditional routine.

A mother's influence should keep pace with the
growth and development of a child. Though principles
remain the same throughout the years, the approach
to a problem or challenge may vary.

Along with these planned times, an alert mother will take advantage of any opportunity to teach a child a lesson right on the spot while the real life situation provides the visual aids and ideal setting. A mother should never be too busy to do this. She should watch for "teaching moments" and, if necessary, create opportunities for the application of lessons on such things as honesty, repentance, forgiveness, gratitude, and thoughtfulness.

A distraught mother said to a friend, "I could be such a good parent if I weren't so darned busy raising kids."

A mother sets the emotional climate in a home. Her attitude and moods are reflected in the lives of those about her. It is easy as you tuck your children in bed each evening and see them as little cherubs to determine: "Tomorrow I will be sweet and pleasant all day long." But to make this last all day long is the challenge. A little boy once asked, "Mommie, why is it that you love me more in the morning than you do at night?"

A choice young mother tells this story:

My grandmother had eleven children, and it seemed as if there was always harmony in her family. I asked my mother one day if she could remember anything specific which might help me to be like her. She said that the incident she remembered best was one time her brothers, who were supposed to be sawing wood, were quarreling. She recalled that her mother was hurrying to prepare a dinner for Church officials, but she stopped and went out and sat on a block of wood near where the boys were sawing, and said the magic words, "Let me tell you a story." My mother said she didn't hear the story, but soon saw her brothers and mother laughing. Later when she went inside, the boys resumed their work without any thought of what they had been quarreling about.

The thought I gleaned from this incident was that my grandmother and mother, too, always took the time to create

the harmony which was in our homes. They always had the
time to listen to our thoughts, to tell us a story, always to be
conscious of our needs.

Music can often be used to encourage harmony in
the home. Peace and beauty seem to be the companions of music, and it is difficult to carry on arguing or
bickering when music can be heard. Early every Sunday morning a lovely mother gets up and begins to
sing. Then as other family members arise, they join
with her in the songs. She says what used to be a hectic
time with everyone rushing to get ready for Sunday
School has now turned into a delightful singing
situation.

Every home should contain songbooks to encourage music enjoyment and appreciation. Music should
be a vital, beautiful part of every child's life. Most
children love to sing and love to be sung to. Many
lessons can be taught through song, and children enjoy
making up silly songs of their own to sing about events
of the day.

Just as music helps set the tone of the home and
can be a medium for teaching, reading and good books
contribute greatly to the life of a child.

The following incident appeared in an issue of
ZCMIRROR, employees publication of ZCMI department store in Salt Lake City:

The little boy's eyes fairly sparkled as he listened to the
funny talking teddy bear introduce himself at the record
center, and he laughed aloud as the bear continued to talk in
his funny voice.

His parents smiled with approval, so the salesperson
thought he might show them how clever the toy really is. The
teddy bear is attached to a record player and has a speaker
inside so little folk can believe he really speaks to them.

There are six teddy bear albums, and other records can
be played on it, too.

The parents didn't seem to have much to say, but they appeared to be pleased with the toy. The mother then took a pad of paper from her handbag and hurriedly wrote a note to the salesman.

He wasn't so surprised—parents often have to be sly when they're doing their Christmas shopping with the young ones along. But this is what the note said:

"We want to get this teddy bear for our little boy. It is really an answer to our prayers. . . . You see, my husband and I are deaf and unable to speak. Now he will be able to hear the bedtime stories we've always wanted to tell him."

How many mothers could read to their children, but don't?

Reading to children first of all makes for wonderful companionship. It teaches children to love books, and it helps them learn to concentrate and listen. Stories develop their imagination and creative thinking. Reading enriches their vocabulary. First grade teachers frequently report that they can always pick

out the students in class who have been read to—they
are ready and eager to learn. Most of all, through the
careful selection of stories, a mother can share with
her children life's treasures and her testimony of
the gospel.

Mothers don't limit your reading just to fairy
tales and the usual type of children's stories. Sometimes we tell our children a special fairy tale about a
king and queen who were blessed with a beautiful little
baby. As the story unfolds, the children realize that
one of them (we tell about each child in turn) is the
beautiful little baby. We believe our children would
rather hear about "when I was a baby" than anything
else we could tell them. This also provides the opportunity to express some deep feelings and project our
thoughts into the future a little. In keeping with the
fairy tale theme, we're able to tell our children how we
love them and how blessed we feel that such choice
spirits have been sent to our home. We tell them of our
dreams and how we, and the Lord, expect them to be
good and great and live beautiful lives. Then as the
story is completed, invariably the child will say, "Oh,
tell me that story again."

Our children love to hear gospel stories, stories
from church history, and faith-promoting incidents.
A number of books are available which help us teach
the gospel to them on their level. You will find gospel
stories on pages 109 to 220.

One of our church leaders was scheduled to address a group of Relief Society workers gathered in the
Tabernacle for conference. At the last minute he was
called out of town, and Elder Matthew Cowley was
invited to take his place. Elder Cowley presented a
masterful sermon on the Book of Mormon. The following day, the Relief Society General President, Sister

Belle S. Spafford, called at Elder Cowley's office to express appreciation for his inspiring talk. She apologized for the very late notice he had been given. Elder Cowley responded: "Late notice? I had plenty of time to prepare that talk. I've been studying for it all my life. My first lesson on the Book of Mormon was at my mother's knee."

> You may have riches and wealth untold,
> Caskets of jewels and baskets of gold,
> But richer than I you will never be,
> For I had a mother who read to me.
> —Thomas Carlyle

President J. Reuben Clark, Jr. said: "Motherhood is the highest type of service mortals know." Mothers, are you worthy of this blessing and responsibility?

FATHER'S INFLUENCE

Puzzle Piece III

*"To be a successful father . . . is greater than to be a success-
ful general or a successful statesman."*

—Joseph Smith

We have never seen the Father here, but have known the Son,
The finest type of manhood, since the world begun.
And summing up the works of God, I write with reverent pen,
The greatest is the Son he sent, to prove the lives of men.
The Lord did not come down himself, to prove to man his
  worth,
He sought our worship through the child He placed here on
  earth.

How can I best express my life; wherein does greatness lie?
How can I long remembrance win, since I am born to die?
Both fame and gold are selfish things; their worth may quickly
  flee,
But I am father of a boy, who came to speak for me.
For someday he shall help the world, long after I am dead.

In all that men may say of him, my praises shall be said.
It matters not what I should gain of fleeting gold and fame,
My hope of joy depends alone on what my boy shall claim.
My story must be told through him, for him I work and plan,
Man's greatest duty is to be—the father of a man.

—Edgar A. Guest

A father is fulfilling great and wonderful responsibilities in helping to create children and in providing materially for them. But, as expressed in the above poem, man's greatest duty is to be the father of a man in the highest sense of the term.

Because it is natural for the mother to spend more time with the children, the rearing of the children is sometimes left up to her entirely. However, it is a grave mistake to underestimate the influence the father has in the lives of his children. He is in a position to set examples and teach in many areas a woman cannot, as well as reinforce the teachings of the mother in the home.

The trend toward equality of women has been essential and beneficial, but in some instances perhaps we have swung too far in the other direction, and some women have assumed more than their share of authority and influence. Some men have been content to let this happen and have sat back and allowed their privileges as head of the family to be taken over by their wives. It is the father who is the head of the house.

As patriarch of the family he has a marvelous opportunity to bring the blessings of the priesthood into his home. It is a father's calling and privilege to lead and direct his family through using his authority in righteousness and in a democratic manner, not as an authoritarian parent. A worthy father will assume this position of influence. Children will never need to be told he is the head of the house—they will grow up

knowing it, and they will love and respect him for it.
They, in turn, will someday establish families of their
own in this same divinely appointed pattern.

We're told in the Bible: "What should it profit
a man if he should gain the whole world, yet lose his
own soul?" We could add: "What should it profit
a father if he should gain the whole world, yet lose his
own child." Surely as Joseph Smith declared, "To be
a successful father is greater than to be a successful
general or a successful statesman." No greater tribute
could be paid a man than to say, "He was a worthy
father."

The responsibility a father faces in providing for
his family materially can never be underestimated. The
numerous problems and difficult decisions a father
must constantly deal with in this area should certainly
increase his family's gratitude to him for the material
blessings he gives them. Along with this, a father is a
faithful companion to his wife as well as kind and loving toward his children. Specifically, how can a father
best express this kindness and love? In what ways can
he exert the greatest influence for good upon his
children?

A father and mother should work *together* in the
disciplining of their children, presenting a united
front always. The father should not leave all the disciplining up to the mother, or vice versa.

One summer day, two little girls were playing outside while their father, just a few feet away, was doing
the never-ending yard work. Soon the father looked
up to see both little girls walking along the rail of a
picket fence, several feet above the ground. If they had
fallen in one direction into the gravel, it would have un-
doubtedly been a painful accident. If they had fallen in
the other direction, the pickets surely would have in-
jured them. Horrified by what he saw, he ran the full

length of the yard, down the driveway, and into the house frantically calling for his wife. As she realized the urgency in his voice, the wife came running to see what was wrong. The panicky father said, "Honey, come quickly and make the girls get off the fence. They might hurt themselves!"

The father should help his children to respect and obey laws by respecting and obeying laws himself.

One time while a family was out riding, the father, in looking for a parking place, pulled alongside a fire hydrant. The father, realizing his mistake, quickly drove away to find another parking place. His little boy asked from the back seat, "Daddy, why didn't you park there?"

The father was preoccupied with other matters and merely answered, "Oh, just because."

What an opportunity that father missed—to explain the purpose of fire hydrants to his son and to help him understand the law which prohibits parking in front of one. What an impressive lesson in obedience to law this could have been to the young boy. This could have been an unforgettable teaching moment.

The well-known naturalist Burroughs said of the great essayist, Ralph Waldo Emerson: "Where he was at all, he was all together." A wise father will concentrate on business and professional matters when he is working, and then when he is at home, he will concentrate on his family. He will take advantage of every opportunity to teach and to talk to and influence his children. If a man is too busy to be a good father, then he is too busy.

A father is in a better position than anyone in the world to teach his children to honor womanhood. The way he speaks to his wife and about her, the way he

treats her, his mother, and other women will be en-
graved deeply upon his children's hearts. A father
who belittles, ridicules, or cheapens womanhood may
pay the price many times over through the actions of
his children. A father who treats his wife with respect,
tenderness, and consideration will reap a rich reward.

An ideal father will help his children value and
appreciate womanhood and their own mother in particular. A fine husband and father we know not only
expresses frequent appreciation to his wife for all she
does, but he also helps his children to be aware of this.
One evening after a delicious dinner, he said, "Children, didn't that taste good? We're surely glad that
Mother is such a good cook." Then he took the children
to their rooms and pointed out their clean, well-pressed
clothing. He called their attention to the orderly house
and the special little touches Mother had added to make
their house a home. He concluded by saying, "We are

so blessed to have Mother. Let us show her how we love her by thanking her for all she does and helping her keep things so nice for us."

A father sets an excellent example for his sons when they see him truly honoring womanhood by making her load a little lighter at times. David Starr Jordan said: "The real heart and soul of a man are measured by the consideration and understanding and respect he shows to women. By a man's ideal of womanhood we may know the degree of his manhood."

A father's esteem for his wife and women in general will set the stage for his son's feelings and actions.

Not only do children need the secure feeling and material blessings which come when a father provides well for his family; they need also to learn lessons for life through his work habits, his ambition, and his values concerning responsibility. Chances are that children will reflect their father's attitude whether one of working just for money or to serve others. A father can teach his children to live for the next holiday just for another day off, or he can help them to look forward to work for the blessing that honest labor is.

A worthy father will reflect through his values that money is a means to an end and not the end within itself. He will not put himself in the bondage of debt so that all his efforts must be spent on meeting material needs. He will proportion his life so there is also time to meet higher needs, such as the cultural and spiritual interests of his family.

Through his example, discussions, and encouragement he can direct his sons toward preparation for a satisfying career. He will help his sons realize that success in a career comes through doing that which provides the most happiness and satisfaction. Psycho-

logical pay should be considered as well as monetary
gain. A father should help his son select a career that
will not only provide for a family's material needs, but
one which will also build him as a person, and will
encourage him to grow and develop his abilities con-
tinually. A well-chosen career should provide the
opportunity truly to serve others and enable one to
keep a proper perspective toward family and church
activities. Pamphlets concerning career opportunities
are available through many business and government
offices.

A father should be wise enough to know when his
family needs a father at home more than an extra
dollar. Money, as merely a status symbol, should not
be his motive. Many families would be happier with
fewer luxuries and more father. Where to draw the
line is a problem that a husband and wife, with the
help of the Lord, will have to evaluate and answer in
their own way. It is a fortunate family that is not
burdened with financial worries beyond reason, and
the importance of being a good provider cannot be
overestimated. However, it must never be forgotten
that "bringing home the bacon" is not a father's sole
responsibility.

Happy relationships between family members are
achieved through a variety of ways. One day a father
and his family of little children were grouped together
in animated conversation. They looked much like a
football team in a huddle on the football field. The
father was later asked what he was telling the children to make them seem so interested and happy. "Oh,
nothing," he said, "I was just listening."

Successful communication between family members is not so much in "telling" as in "listening and
understanding."

Does your conversation consist only of "uh-huh" or can you respond enthusiastically to enthusiasm? Can you respond with love and understanding to problems? Do you have the empathy to put yourself in the shoes of your child and really know how he feels? Are you easy to talk to? Are you fun to talk to? Are you responsive? Can you joke, tease, and laugh together? Are you demonstrative enough to give a child a feeling of security? Is your interest felt? Is your love felt? Is your understanding felt?

Remember, communication is a two-way street. It is one of the most important thoroughfares between parent and child.

Fathers cannot afford to be too busy to help children with their problems or to be too impatient or too hurried to do something with them.

There is nothing I love to see more than my husband and children going somewhere together, hand in hand. Perhaps they are going only to the grocery store or sometimes they have a more adventuresome destination such as a merry-go-round ride at the park or a trip to the air terminal to watch planes take off and land. The destination is only secondary to the companionship and togetherness they are experiencing.

It is said that "the thing most apt to drive a parent wild is a child behaving like a child!" When your youngsters become your shadow and follow you from place to place to "help" you as you are trying to catch up on yardwork or household chores and repairs, there will likely be some exasperating moments. But a father who takes the time and patience to share his life with his children will have rewards richer than he could hope for, because they will then want to share their lives with him!

Actually, it isn't a question of how much time you put in with a child, but what you put into the time that counts. O. A. Battista said, "The best inheritance a parent can give his child is a few minutes of his time each day."

The things you plan to do with your children will be determined by your time, your interests, your finances, and your location. But don't make the mistake of waiting only for big things to come along. Ten minutes a day of real companionship with your children will have a far greater influence on their lives than two or three spectacular activities during a year's time.

One morning my small son said to me at breakfast, "Daddy, may I read to you? I got nine out of ten for reading at school yesterday."

"Very good," said I, hardly glancing from my paper.

"May I?"

"Eh? May you what?" I demanded—being in haste, and wishful to glance over the news and finish breakfast in next to no time.

"May I read to you?"

"Well, not now, son! There's no time!"

So off I went to catch a bus.

Home that evening, I told my little son that I would listen to his reading as soon as I had had my supper. But somebody called, and I had to see him. And then somebody else called, and I had to engage him. And finally I went into my son's bedroom, and found him fast asleep, his cheeks wet with tears, a school reader open on the bed.

Thus, through this experience, I learned my lesson: to love him a little more and myself a little less.

Of course children look forward to doing special things—the trips to the amusement park, the circus, swimming excursions, canyon hikes, and vacations.

But it is also a real treat to have Daddy read the bed-time story occasionally, or to have him take time to visit in a man-to-man fashion with a young son or provide an opportunity for a confidential talk with a teenage daughter.

One Sunday afternoon a father took his four-year-old boy to his room for a nap. The father lay down by his son for a little while and told him how he loved him and how proud he was to have him for a son. He expressed his feelings along this line for awhile and then asked, "Son, how do you feel about us? Are you happy here?" The little boy replied that he was very happy and that he really loved his mother and daddy and four sisters.

Then the father asked, "Is there anything else we could do for you to make you happy?"

The child quickly answered, "Yes, I would surely like a little brother to play with!"

It is good to talk together and learn how they feel and what they want.

Life brings perplexing and disturbing problems to young people (not that older folks are exempt), and they sometimes grope feverishly for help. Too often they do not know to whom to turn, and yet if we picture an ideal father in our minds, one of the first things we think of is an understanding man sharing his wisdom and giving counsel to his children. It is a shame that all children do not turn more readily to their parents than they sometimes do. The fault certainly lies partly with the children, but perhaps we as parents share more of the blame than we would like to admit. Maybe the problem had its roots in early years when our two-year-old's problems seemed so insignificant to us that we treated them too lightly.

The two-year-old quickly learned to go somewhere else for sympathy and advice.

Do we take the time and effort to see things through the eyes of our children? Can the father understand that a toddler's cut finger, an adolescent boy's failure to make the school football team, or a teenage daughter's having no date to the big school dance are as disastrous in their eyes as a serious financial loss would be to him?

One young girl spent hours crying because the doctor told her after a serious operation that she wouldn't be able to dance at the school Valentine dance. Some adults and parents would be inclined to say, in such a situation, "Oh, don't be silly. You're young. There are many more dancing years ahead for you." A wiser, more understanding parent would have exercised empathy and said, "I understand how you feel. It really is a disappointment to miss this special occasion. Would it help you to go watch or would you prefer to have a few of your friends over sometime for an ice cream party or something?"

When children can find understanding and sympathy, along with wisdom, in their father, a close companionship can develop. And children can readily tell the difference between genuine interest in their affairs and mock interest.

Fathers cannot afford to be too busy to help children with their problems or too impatient to understand them. It is a wonderful feeling to me to know that even, now, if it were necessary, I could turn to my father for advice and feel assured he would give me the best counsel available.

A child must not only be understood; he needs to be accepted by his father. Sometimes children get the impression that they are not.

Fathers are large people
  Who frequently declare
That "other children" eat their meals
  And sit straight on a chair.
"Other children" wash their hands
  According to my father.

They never yell, or lose their hats
  Or fight, or be a bother.
"Other children," Father says
  Speak when they're spoken to.
They answer "Please" and "Thank You"
  The way I'm s'posed to do.

I'm sorry for my father,
  Just as sorry as can be;
He knows such lovely children
  'n' gets stuck with one like me.
                —Zoa Sherburne

    An ideal father will support his children in their activities. Whenever they perform in public, from Junior Sunday School days on, it makes them feel special, and it gives them confidence and a burning desire to do their best to know that their parents are interested enough to be present. The father, as well as the mother, should also become acquainted with the children's teachers and support the P.T.A.

    A wise father will do more than just tolerate family activities and traditions; he will support them actively and enthusiastically. He might be ready with a camera to make pictorial records of special occasions. It is a tradition at our home to make birthday cakes in special shapes and designs. Mother bakes the cakes—with the help of the children—but it is Daddy who often plans the design and cuts the cake accordingly. Daddy's contributions add so much to the memory and fun of it all.

Along with ideals, examples, teachings, and moments to remember, a father could pass along some tangible things for his children to treasure. How we love the post cards our father sent us while he was away at army camps. The little cupboard, cedar chest, and other doll furniture he made for us will always be prized possessions; in fact, little grandchildren are now enjoying and playing with them. A father's favorite book handed down or the pocketknife he had as an Eagle Scout passed on could mean so much in the lives of children.

Do you remember as a child when you were sure your father was the most handsome man in the world; that only he knew how to select a perfect Christmas tree; and he was the only person who knew how to repair broken toys? We were brought up knowing that "our daddy can do everything." A mother should help her children gain this love and confidence in their father. A good father will live to be worthy of that image. Through the children's experiences they will learn that their father's advice is sound; that the solutions he gives to problems work out; and that the repaired toys run again.

Even though the father must live to merit this love and confidence, he must never give his children the impression that he is perfect, that he is always right, and that he never makes mistakes. Everyone makes mistakes. These mistakes won't necessarily shatter the trust children have. Instead they can endear the father to the children, particularly when they see that their father is a big enough man to admit that he was wrong and can apologize for being so.

As children we lived in the Southern States while our father was stationed at an army camp. One time we toured a tobacco plant. We were very young at the time and remember nothing about the tour of the plant. But we do remember being in the office after the tour when my father was offered a complimentary cigar. He refused it, saying he had never smoked in his life. This seemed incredible to the guide, and even though we were young, we could tell from his reaction that it was indeed unusual to encounter a man who had never smoked. The pride we felt will long be remembered as we saw our father live up to his standards.

If only fathers could realize the influence they exert through their attitudes and examples toward sacred matters and ideals! The father's attitude toward church attendance and church activity will most likely be assumed by the children, particularly the young boys, as they grow up. Children are quick to perceive a parent's true feelings. True spirituality is reflected in the lives of the children.

Only a father can bring his family the blessings of the priesthood. The father is the patriarch of his family and through that order comes the priesthood. What a blessing it is for a family to have as their father one who truly honors that priesthood and who uses it to lead his family in righteousness, as designed by our Father in heaven.

Those of us living in Latter-day Saint homes have more reason than any other people on earth to show the father respect and to honor him as head of the household. It is through him that the Holy Priesthood of God is brought into the home. If this priesthood is being honored as it should be, there is no greater blessing we can ask for. We know that the Lord is constantly blessing us with inspiration and revelation. The father, as head of the home, has every right to receive this inspiration regarding the affairs of his family. With the complex living of today and the many family problems and crises that arise, how desperately we need this guidance. Fathers, are you in tune with the Lord so that he can direct your actions?

It is important that Latter-day Saint fathers take seriously their opportunity to perform the ordinances of the Church where their children are involved. We feel extremely blessed, when looking over our church records, to see that our father has been worthy to perform these ordinances in our lives. What an honor it is to have our father give us a name and blessing. This is a father's right and privilege. We are thrilled to see our father's name on our baptismal and confirmation records. Our brothers are grateful to have been ordained to the various offices in the priesthood by their father.

One of the great moments in a mother's life is to see her husband take their little baby in his arms and give the child a name and blessing. This is a sacred experience; heaven seems so very close at such a time.

A father should administer to a family member who is ill so that the blessings of the Lord can strengthen the medical help available. A father could ask a special blessing when someone in the family is leaving for a trip, going away to school or the service, departing for the mission field, anticipating a challenging assignment, or is trying to conquer a serious problem.

A father should bear his testimony to his wife and children through his every word and deed. They should see him stand on his feet and express his feelings for the gospel.

Children will be blessed, now and forever, by having their father declare, as did Joshua of old, "As for me and my house, we will serve the Lord."

FAMILY PRAYER

PUZZLE PIECE IV

"Prayer should be the key of the day and the lock of the night."
—English Proverb

A number of years ago I went into the County Hospital in Salt Lake City for the purpose of administering to the sick. Lying on a bed was a boy nine years old, a charity patient of whom I had heard. He was emaciated and had pneumonia, among other things. I said, "Lawrence, do you feel very sick?"

He answered, "Yes."

I said, "Have you suffered much pain?"

"Awful pain," he replied.

I said, "Have you asked the Lord to take the pain away?"

The little fellow looked up in amazement and said, "I don't know how."

He had never been taught to pray. He had never been taught that there is a power greater than man's power. I explained to him that he could ask the Lord to bless him. Then we asked the Lord to bless him.

I asked myself this question: "How many homes are there where husband and wife, father and mother, understand the gospel? How many children growing up in those homes do not know how to pray?"

A few days after that, I heard of another nine-year-old boy, an orphan, who was hurried off to the hospital where examination indicated that he had to be operated upon without delay. He had been living with friends who had given him a. home. His father and mother (when they were alive) had taught him to pray. Thus, when he came to the hospital, the thing he wanted was to have the Lord help him.

The doctors had decided to hold a consultation. When he was wheeled into the operating room, he looked around and saw the nurses and the doctors who had consulted on his case. He knew that it was very serious and he said to one of them as they were preparing to give him the anesthetic: "Doctor, before you begin to operate, won't you please pray for me?"

The doctor, with seeming embarrassment, offered his excuses and said, "I can't pray for you." Then the boy asked the other doctors, with the same result.

Finally, something very remarkable happened. This little fellow said, "If you can't pray for me, will you please wait while I pray for myself?"

They removed the sheet, and he knelt on the operating table, bowed his head and said, "Heavenly Father, I am only an orphan boy. I am awful sick. Won't you please make me well? Bless these men who are going to operate that they will do it right. If you will, make me well and I will try to grow up to be a good man. Thank you, Heavenly Father, for making me well."

When he got through praying, he lay down. The doctors' and the nurses' eyes filled with tears. Then he said, "I am ready."

The operation was performed. The little fellow was taken back to his room and in a few days they took him from the hospital, well on the way to complete recovery.

Some days after that a man who had heard of the incident went to the office of one of the surgeons and said, "Tell me about the operation you performed a few days ago—the operation on a little boy."

The surgeon said, "I have operated on several little boys."

The man added, "This little boy wanted someone to pray for him."

The doctor said very seriously, "There was such a case but I don't know but that it is too sacred a thing for me to talk about."

The man said, "Doctor, if you will tell me, I will treat it with respect. I would like to hear it."

Then the doctor told the story about as I have told it here, and added: "I have operated on hundreds of people, men and women, who thought they had faith to be healed. But never until I stood over that little boy have I felt the presence of God as I felt it then. That boy opened the windows of heaven and talked to his Heavenly Father as one would talk to another face to face. I want to say to you that I am a better man for having had this experience of standing and hearing a little boy talk to his Father in heaven as if he were present."

"Remember there is a God in heaven—and parents . . . shall . . . teach their children to pray, and to walk uprightly before the Lord." (D&C 68:28.)

—Lucy Gertsch Thomson
Treasured Stories

Family prayers lay the foundation in the lives of children for faith, testimonies, closeness to the Lord, missions, and temple marriages. Children who learn the power of prayer will know countless blessings.

We have found that our young children pray more willingly if we help them feel that their turn to pray is a real privilege. Their daddy calls on them by saying something like this, "Diane, you were the first one on your knees this morning. You may pray for us." Or, "Jean, we would like you to pray today. You surely have been a sweet girl."

To help them gain the confidence they need to pray for the family, we have devoted a number of family home evenings to a lesson on prayer, like the one on page 177. We have found also that our "Happiest

Experience" routine as previously mentioned, helps them to have things in mind to pray about.

A special time and place for family prayer should be designated. If we don't take time for the Lord, how can we expect him to take time for us? All distractions should be shut out, and an attitude of reverence and worship should be reflected by the family members. A family should kneel together in prayer at least once a day. Brigham Young said:

> Say your prayers always before going to work. Never forget that. A father—the head of the family—should never miss calling his family together and dedicating himself and them to the Lord of Hosts, asking the guidance and direction of his Holy Spirit to lead them through the day—that very day. Lead us this day, guide us this day, preserve us this day, save us from sinning against thee or any being in heaven or on earth this day! If we do this every day, the last day we live we will be prepared to enjoy a higher glory.
>
> (*Journal of Discourses* 12:261.)

If family circumstances prevent this early morning devotion, prayer should be held regularly at some other time, and every family member should also be taught to pray in private.

Family prayers should not be unduly lengthy. If a prayer is too long, children become restless, and they are inclined to become resentful about praying.

The family prayer should be meaningful to the children. The terminology should be such that they can follow the thoughts, and the subjects should be of interest to them and concern their welfare. Children should hear themselves mentioned by name in the prayers.

If parents pray simply, children will feel more encouraged to pray. When a child does pray, his efforts should be commended. He should be praised, particularly, when his prayers express his own thoughts rather than just what he has heard others say.

Children should grow up knowing that we don't just ask for more blessings in prayer. An ideal prayer is basically one of gratitude; thanks to the Lord for life and all the bounties thereof.

Children should learn that instead of asking the Lord for favors, we should pray for the strength, ability, and wisdom to work out many of our blessings. Also, children should understand that we do not pray and then forget about the matter; our Father in heaven expects us to do everything we can to answer our own prayers and then he will supplement our efforts.

The single act of family prayer can do more for the spiritual security of the family than any other thing you can do. Family prayer is an essential element in preparing for eternal family life.

Family prayer unites a family physically—they are all together in one place. It can do much for uniting a family spiritually—forever.

President Heber J. Grant gave us his testimony of family prayer:

I am convinced that one of the greatest things that can come into any home to cause the boys and girls in that home to grow up in a love of God, and in a love of the gospel of Jesus Christ, is to have family prayer. It is not for the father of the family alone to pray, but for the mother and for the children to do so also, that they may partake of the spirit of prayer, and be in harmony, be in tune, to have the radio, so to speak, in communication with the Spirit of the Lord. I believe that there are very few who go astray, that very few lose their faith, who have once had a knowledge of the gospel, and who never neglect their prayers in their families, and their secret supplications to God.

(*Conference Report,* October 1923.)

Wise parents should help children to understand and accept answers to prayers.

Sometimes the answer is "yes."

A young woman who served as secretary to one of the General Authorities recalls this incident: "Early one morning as this General Authority returned to his office briefly between two traveling assignments, he was very eager to take care of a great deal of correspondence. He told me that right after lunch he would dictate a number of letters. I felt absolutely heartsick. For several days I had been suffering from a terrible pain in the tendons of my wrist, and it was absolutely impossible for me to grip a pen. But I knew that those letters had to be written, and so I prayed fervently to the Lord to bless me that I would be able to do my part. I prayed several times during the course of the morning, and even though my wrist still throbbed, I just knew that the blessing would be granted. As I returned from lunch, he called me into his office. I will never forget that walk; the pain in my wrist was nearly excruciating as I practised holding my pen. As I sat in the chair by his desk, the pain completely left my wrist, and I was able to take dictation for over an hour. I knew that the Lord had heard and answered my prayer."

Children must learn that sometimes the answer is "no."

A little girl had prayed for sunshine so that she could have an outdoor birthday party. The day of the party came, and it rained hard all day long. The little girl cried bitterly, and in her disappointment blamed the Lord for not answering her prayers. Her mother explained that perhaps the farmers, too, had been praying and that they had prayed for rain. Perhaps the Lord had felt it more important that the crops have moisture than that she have good weather for a party.

Sometimes the answer is just a way to work it out for ourselves.

On an icy, wintry day in Montana, a stagecoach was cracking its way over the frozen earth. Inside the coach the passengers, a woman and her tiny baby, were suffering from the intense cold. The mother had bowed her head in prayer and removed her coat to cover the baby. The driver observed that she was now showing dangerous signs of drowsiness. He stopped the coach, asked the woman to step on the ground a moment, and as she did so, he whipped the horses and the coach was off, leaving the lady standing on the road. Of course she was panic stricken and ran after the coach screaming and calling desperately for her child. After a little while the driver stopped and waited for the frantic woman to catch up. He then gently helped her back in the coach, tenderly placed the baby back on her lap, and resumed the journey.

Sometimes the answer is so indirect that we fail to recognize it.

An old colored man was shingling a roof and slipped and began rolling toward the edge. As the ground was rushing up to meet him, he offered a frantic prayer to the Lord to be saved. Just about that time his overalls caught on a nail. He quickly added, "Nevah mind, Lawd; I'm ah right nauw."

Children should learn from others' experiences as well as their own, that there is power in prayer.

On the night of April 14, 1912, I was working late on the copy desk of my alma mater, the old Baltimore *American*. It was long after midnight when I put away my eyeshade and made ready to go home. Suddenly Dr. Shipley, our night editor, rushed to the inside telephone and called downstairs:

"Stop the presses! A great liner has hit an iceberg in mid-ocean!"

There was no going home then; the tragedy of the *Titanic* was the news of the year. Out of that disaster came many epics of individual heroism—the way Mrs. Isidor Strauss refused place in a lifeboat, to die with her husband; the calm courage with which Charles Frohman greeted death as "the great adventure." But to me the greatest of all these heartbreaking episodes was the extraordinary fate of Colonel Archibald Gracie.

That remarkable story has its scenes on sea and on land. The colonel's wife was not voyaging with him; she was waiting for him in New York, where, as I recall it, she was a guest in the house of friends. Late that Sunday evening, Mrs. Gracie was reading in bed and fell asleep with her book. Suddenly others in the house heard a piercing cry.

Rushing into the bedroom, they found Mrs. Gracie in a distracted state. While dreaming, she had heard her husband's voice calling to her, pleading for her prayers. Now wide awake, she was overwhelmed with a deep and terrible feeling of danger, a sense of disaster so deep, so real, so undeniable, that the frightened wife resisted all efforts to calm her.

She knelt beside the bed and began to pray, and there she knelt and continued to pray for the rest of the night. Dawn came before she rose, but now her agitation was gone. Her soul was full of peace, and she went quickly to sleep.

But there was no peace in the rest of the household. At early breakfast that morning, host and hostess were confounded to see the gaunt black headlines—the *Titanic* on her maiden crossing had crashed into an iceberg and was now at the bottom of the sea. Hundreds, perhaps thousands, of lives were lost. That host and his wife could not speak to each other; could hardly look at each other. For they remembered Mrs. Gracie's nightmare; the voice she had heard in her uneasy dream. And they knew that Colonel Gracie was a passenger on the *Titanic*. How could they bring themselves to tell her?

When they did tell her, they were astonished at her calmness. Gone were the fears of the night; with perfect serenity she told her friends: "I am not afraid. All is well with my loved one. I know it in my soul."

But how could it be well with Colonel Gracie? The life-
boats were all too few and some of them were smashed, and
the way was cleared for women and children first. After
helping them into the boats, Colonel Gracie went up to the
hurricane deck, there to await the end. He knew it would not
be long before the ship went down; he could feel its death
shudders already. And when the vessel began to sink, he
resolved to leap clear and not go down with her, to die fighting
for life.

That was a high dive for an aging man. When he struck
the icy water, he plunged deep and far, holding his breath until
his lungs seemed ready to burst. That was when he prayed;
that was when the cry went out of his heart to his wife and
up to God, beseeching prayer and salvation. It was a spontaneous imploring from the soul, full of love and power.

When he rose to the surface, grasping, he saw floating
nearby a rail from a broken box crate. For a little while
he clung to it and then, soon, in the misty light, he made out a
raft. It was overloaded and partly under water, but its occu-
pants pulled him up with them. As they stood on the crazy
thing, rising and falling with the waves, they prayed, each
man in his own tongue.

And before the day was over, the word went winging to
the wife ashore that all was as her prayers had made her
sure it would be—her loved one was safe and coming home
to her.

"The Call In The Dark"
copyright 1951 by Fulton Oursler
from *Modern Parables,* by Fulton Oursler
Reprinted by Permission of Doubleday &
Company, Inc.

As children are taught to pray, they should learn
that the Lord loves them dearly and that the answers,
whatever they may be, are for their ultimate good
and blessing.

Children should gain the desire to go to the Lord
with their problems. Parents and children should
kneel together and ask the Lord's blessings and help
when special problems or challenges arise. Children

should grow in the faith that sometimes only our Father in heaven knows the answer. They should talk with him daily.

And as a family joins together in prayer, the children should feel, as did Heber J. Grant as a small boy. He often played with the children of Brigham Young and on many occasions he would join in family prayers at the Young home. He recalled that more than once he would glance up to where President Young was praying to see if the Lord was standing there. When President Young prayed, his children felt that the Lord was right there in the room. Family prayer should be just that personal and real.

May we as parents adhere to the counsel in the Book of Mormon when the Savior said: "Pray in your families unto the father in my name, that your wives and your children may be blessed." (3 Nephi 18:21.)

DINNER
TABLE
DISCUSSIONS

PUZZLE PIECE V

Success can begin at a dining table!

How would you like to have a tape recorder placed in your dining room, making a record of all that is said at your dinner table? Would the recording sound something like this?

Mother: "Do you know what I heard this morning? Sue told me that she heard that the Joneses only have to pay half as much as we do on their ward building fund. And just last week they put new carpeting in their living room and finished their patio, and their car is a much newer model than ours. It just isn't fair. We could surely use a new carpet, but with all that money to pay. . . . Nothing's fair around here."

* * *

Or would the conversation go like this:

Father: "How was school today, Ralph?"

Ralph: "Oh, that third period is really a mess. Miss Adams hasn't got a brain in her head. I don't know why the school board doesn't consider her a charity case and let her retire five years early. I'm just glad the year's almost over. I feel sorry for you, Sharon, having her to look forward to next year. She won't be able to teach you a thing."

* * *

What about this type of discussion:

Mother: "I don't know why you can never get to the table on time. It seems that all I do is wait, and after how hard I've worked, too."

Father: "Well, if you ever served anything different maybe there'd be some reason to get here. What have we got tonight? Oh, not a casserole again. Can't you think of anything better to fix than that?"

Mother: "Now, listen. If you made more money and gave me enough to live on, maybe I could fix something decent. Besides, you don't ever help me sit down like my father always used to do for Mother. Johnny, stop acting so silly and start eating your dinner!"

* * *

You would feel more pleased if the tape recorder revealed something more like the following conversation at your dinner table.

Father: "Today I know how Adam must have felt."

Mother: "How's that, dear?"

Father: "I had opposition in all things! Everything I had to do was a real test of my fortitude and patience. But it gives me a great deal of satisfaction to come home tired, yet feeling good inside for being able to work those problems out successfully. How was your day, John?"

John: "Pretty good, I guess. That cute girl who sits next to me in seminary said 'Hi' to me."

Father: "That's good news. What did your seminary teacher say that was interesting?"

John: "We talked about our destiny as Latter-day Saints and how we are a covenant people with a real purpose in life and a responsibility to the rest of the world. I'd never thought of it in that way before, and it really made me think."

Father: "And what did he say was your responsibility, John?"

John: "He said that a part of my responsibility was to go on a mission and give others the opportunity of hearing the gospel. It really made me enthusiastic to fulfil a mission."

Father: "I'm glad you're thinking seriously now about it, John. You know that Mom and I are behind you in this 100 percent, and we'll help you in any way you want. Actually, this would be a good time to make some definite plans regarding the things you need to study during the next few years to prepare you. Perhaps we could do that tonight and maybe calculate how much more money you think you'll be able to earn for your mission fund in the next few years."

"How was your day, Susan?"

Susan: "I had a lot of fun today except for Mrs. Knowlton's class. She expects us to memorize 50 lines from Macbeth. I don't see what good that will do us."

Mother: "I remember when I was in school I felt the same way about English, Susan. But as I look back over my life, I've learned to appreciate the teachers who made me work hard. Nothing worth having comes easy in life, including the ability to speak or write. I'm sure that someday you'll be as grateful to Mrs. Knowlton as I am to my teachers."

* * *

Part of your children's education will be gained at the dining room table. What are they going to learn? Are you going to teach them how to criticize and gossip; how to argue and complain; how to be a little on the shady side regarding honesty. Or will they learn to see and appreciate fine things by creating an atmosphere conducive to wholesome attitudes toward life, true understanding and appreciation of people, a high regard for ecclesiastical and civil authorities, and healthy feelings towards morals, values, and ideals?

Parents should first set the stage for an edifying dinner hour by serving a dinner which has been planned in advance, prepared with loving care, and served attractively and on time. A well set table, rather than one where the plates and silverware have been carelessly thrown around, adds so much to the right type of atmosphere. Then the family prayer or a blessing helps the dinner hour get off to the right start.

Dinner table conversations should not be rigid or preachy or too planned. They should be natural and spontaneous and even include good humor and fun. Parents should evaluate the conversation periodically during the course of the dinner and guide it along a high plane. They should encourage constructive questions and answers and subtly turn the conversation toward edifying, educational topics.

Parents should be careful not to talk over the heads of the children at the table. Care should be given, too, to see that one family member doesn't monopolize the entire conversation. As much as possible, the dinner table conversation should be of interest to everyone present and should include everyone in turn. A pleasant dinner hour could do much to help cure the American rush and dash problem and could be the highlight in a family's day.

Ideas for table conversation topics might include current events, which is really history in the making. The activities of family members—events at work and school—could be stimulating and interesting. Discussions about family projects, such as building a new family room, could be educational and help promote family co-operation and togetherness. A review of Sunday School and Primary lessons would be most worthwhile. Perhaps the speaker's message in Sacrament meeting could be discussed in a positive manner. Each family member might mention what he or she gained from the talk. Even if the speaker was not outstanding, perhaps his spirit or humility was impressive.

Mealtime provides an opportunity for parents to visit with their children and counsel them. A fine father addresses each child individually during the course of breakfast and tries to say something which will help him or her that day, such as: "Steve, how did your studies go last evening? I'm sure you will do your best with the exam today." And, "You surely look lovely in your new dress, Becky."

Some special mealtime projects could prove of great value to a family. One family I know learns a new word each day, and then the last day of the week they review all the words and practise using them. Special lessons on manners and table etiquette would also be appropriate for mealtime discussion. See page 138 for ideas along this line.

Some families set aside five minutes or so after either breakfast or dinner to read a few pages from a book. Think what five minutes of reading each day could mean over a period of five years, or ten years. If the ages of the children vary greatly, humorous and animal stories can appeal to everyone and bring about a successful family reading project.

A few minutes at mealtime might be devoted to the memorization of a scripture, learning an article of faith, knowing the names of the General Authorities and their order in the governing bodies of the Church. The books of the Bible and the Book of Mormon could be learned this same way. When we lived in the mission home in Holland, we would go around the table, each person taking part by saying the next book of the Bible, the order of the members of the Council of the Twelve, a passage from the scriptures, and so on.

A wonderful contribution to a happy, successful family life would be wisely directed dinner table discussions. In this way family members could learn from one another; good characters could be molded; and parents could make use of one of their best opportunities to influence their children.

Remember, success can begin at your dining room table, particularly if this sound advice from the story of Bambi is your motto:

"If you can't say somethin' nice, don't say nothin' at all."

MOMENTS
TO
REMEMBER

PUZZLE PIECE VI

"People become the sum total of the experiences they have had."

Four little cousins were busily playing in Grandmother's back yard on the swings and in the sandpile, each one thoroughly occupied with his particular activity. About midmorning, Grandma came to the back door and simply called "cracker time." The immediate result was that all four children dropped whatever they were doing and ran to sit, side by side, on the big red lawn swing, full of anticipation for the treat Grandma was bringing them.

Actually it was only soda crackers for each one—
a sensible mid-morning snack to keep tiny tummies
from getting too hungry before lunch time. And what
grandmother isn't delighted to treat her grandchildren to crackers, cookies, or other goodies? But this
very wise grandmother turned a routine event into a
special occasion, and to these four little cousins
"cracker time" is already a wonderful part of
their lives.

Someday when they reach adulthood, it will take
only an insignificant soda cracker to bring to their
minds a flood of beautiful memories of times shared
together with dear cousins at Grandma's house. This
has already become a tradition—a moment to remember—in their young lives and "cracker time" has
joined closer together four little hearts—no, five
hearts, for Grandma is certainly a part of this—and
nourished a love for each other that will remain precious over the years. And it will be many times more
difficult for these children to forget the principles and
teachings of their home when just a common soda
cracker will remind them of the people and the experiences that influenced their young lives with goodness and beauty.

Creating and cherishing moments to remember
can contribute so much to good times as children grow
up; moments to remember provide an ideal way to
bind the family closely to the things in life which are
precious and important; they help to recall lessons
and values learned; and they will bring about rewarding experiences which may influence your family
forever.

Almost all families fall into a few traditions
throughout their lives, but many families make the
extra effort to create memorable events in the lives

of children. Giving children these occasions is like taking out "love insurance" with them.

We let so many opportunities slip by us—we so often just hand each child a soda cracker while he is playing instead of taking an extra minute and having a "cracker time." But what an immeasurable difference and effect on the life of a child between a soda cracker and a "cracker time!"

A tradition—or moment to remember—need not be spectacular in order to be impressive. Some very simple, yet meaningful, experiences enrich the lives of children. A bedtime story, a "Happiest Experience" time, as previously mentioned, the blessing before meals, strolling through the park hand in hand, Mother's smile first thing in the morning and last thing at night—these are the things which make families firm and substantial. They give solid roots in the past and hopes for the future. They are little things by themselves but put together they spell solidarity in family life.

Your children in turn will probably perpetuate some of these same traditions in their own families, thus giving you a common bond with grandchildren and great-grandchildren. As parents, be alert to new ideas for moments to remember and be conscious of the fine things you already do so that your children will grow up with treasured memories or "love insurance."

Holidays naturally lend themselves to family traditions. Valentines, Easter, Mother's Day and Father's Day, Memorial Day, the Fourth of July, Halloween—all of these occasions bring moments to remember.

Thanksgiving is the most traditional of all American holidays. In our family we always have a large group of relatives together to enjoy the traditional turkey, dressing, cranberries, hot rolls, yams, salads, and pumpkin pie. Even the dishwashing afterwards is always more fun than work, giving us a chance for informal chatter we sometimes don't take the time for throughout the year. But the best part of the day is the program that comes after dinner as both little children and grown-ups share their talents in the form of music and verse, skits, and storytelling. Among all the fun, laughter, food, games, and entertainment, the real purpose of the day is always preserved through prayers of gratitude, beautiful readings, stories, and songs to remind us of Thanksgiving and its significance. One impressive tradition is to have everyone present name that which he has been most grateful for during the past year. Sometimes a special tribute could be paid to the grandparents present for the heritage and blessings they have given the family. Thanksgiving should be much more than just a family reunion. Make it a treasured, spiritual, upbuilding experience in the lives of everyone.

Then just four weeks later comes Christmas. Moments to remember are synonymous with Christmas. Along with the good times which accompany Santa Claus, trees, gifts, and goodies, a family will encourage other traditions.

It is good to shift the emphasis from "what am I going to get" to "what can I make or do for someone else." Very early in life a child can learn that it is more blessed to give than to receive if he has parents who are willing to teach him this lesson by letting him create things for others. It is much more work and takes a great deal more patience to help a child in this than it does to give him a dollar and send him to the store to choose a gift for someone. But a parent who

is conscientiously attempting to teach his children
great lessons cannot afford to let this opportunity
slip by.

At holiday time a family can have fun decorating and filling cookie buckets, baking gingerbread men,
or making other treats and giving them to family
members and friends.

After decorating the tree, rather than just rou-
tinely turning on the lights, why not gather the family together to sing a favorite carol as the lights are
turned on for the first time. It would be a little thing
to do but what a big difference it could make!

A traditional family song, "Hang up the Baby's
Stocking," is reproduced on pages 64 and 65.

Christmas Eve is an ideal time to hold the grand-
est family night of the year. Special programs to help
children catch the true spirit of Christmas should be
held. Perhaps family members can dramatize the
story of the first Christmas with bathrobes, towels,
and scarves for the shepherds. A new baby or a favorite doll could portray the Baby Jesus. The second
chapter in the book of Luke could provide the narra-
tive. The Christmas story depicted on a flannelboard
could also be impressive.

Here is a simple tradition which can become
meaningful and enjoyable to a family. After the
young children have gone to bed, the grown-ups play
"Santa Claus" and visit. Just before retiring for the
night (it is usually about midnight by this time) the
father opens the front door to welcome Christmas in.

We have a "Christmas Counter" at our home (see illustration). We hang it up the first day of December and each day throughout the month a little pocket is opened, revealing a decoration for the tree on the right or a figure to complete the manger scene on the left. This is such a fun way to help children anticipate Christmas and answer the persistent question: "How many more days until Christmas?"

Birthdays, like Christmas, are special times and call for special activities. One time a little girl, Sharilyn, insisted on mailing herself a birthday card. It seemed almost all of her playmates were having birthdays that time of year and she just couldn't wait until hers came. Birthdays are very important to children and should be treasured events each year. Don't just crowd these days into your daily routine; make them live in the memories of your children.

OH! HANG UP THE BABY'S STOCKING

author of words unknown   music arranged by Ellen F. Bentley

Oh, hang up the ba-by's stock-ing. Be sure that you do not forget.

For the dear lit-tle dim-pled darling, Has nev-er seen Christ-mas yet.

We've told her all a-bout it. She o-pened her big blue eyes.

I'm sure she un-der-stood it. For she looked so cun-ning and wise.

Hang up the Baby's Stocking

Oh, hang up the baby's stocking.
Be sure that you do not forget,
For the dear little dimpled darling,
Has never seen Christmas yet.
We've told her all about it.
She opened her big blue eyes.
I'm sure she understood it,
For she looked so cunning and wise.

Oh, I know what we'll do for the baby
I've thought of the very best plan
We'll borrow a stocking from granny
The very largest we can,
And hang it by her dear mother's
Right here in the corner so.
And write a letter to Santa
And fasten it on to the toe.

Write:

This is the baby's stocking
That hangs in the corner here
She hasn't seen you yet, Santa,
For she only came this year.
But she's just the blessedest baby
And now before you go
Just cram her stocking with goodies
From the top clear down to the toe.
Oh, hang up the baby's stocking
Be sure that you do not forget
For the dear little dimpled darling
Has never seen Christmas yet.

(author unknown)

At birthday time our children are always "king" or "queen" for the day and are privileged to select their very favorite dishes for dinner.

Along with this, tiny children love to have a special cake. It might be shaped like a merry-go-round or a choo-choo train frosted to fit specifications or a cake shaped like a dog, butterfly, airplane, or doll. This is even more fun if the children are allowed to help with the baking and decorating.

Along with birthday dinners, one parent could give a "sermonette" and express appreciation for the child. Or each member of the family, in turn, might pay a tribute to the birthday person.

The Dutch people have a wonderful birthday custom. The person celebrating his birthday always sends a lovely bouquet of flowers to his mother to express gratitude to her for bringing him into the world.

If your family is closely tied to a particular foreign country, you may want to incorporate into your American life some favorite foreign holidays, traditions, or customs. You can enrich your children's cultural heritage in this manner as well as their understanding and appreciation of people from other lands.

Daily happenings can become tremendously important as they are repeated. My husband never leaves the house without a hug and a kiss for each child; if he should ever forget, the whole thing is treated as a major tragedy!

One of the General Authorities tells of a custom they have in their home no matter how old their children become. Whenever the children come home after a date, a social event, or any activity, they always kiss their parents goodnight, even though the parents

may already be in bed. This custom has several pur-
poses. It assures the parents that the children are
home safely for the night; it creates a bond of love in
the family; and it serves as a safeguard to the children
for they would never dare come home with alcohol
or tobacco on their breath, knowing they will kiss their
parents goodnight.

Enjoying creative fun—everything from finger
painting to papier maché—is a traditional part of our
home. The "creations" are displayed on a large bulletin board in our family room, and then later the
choicest works of all are selected for the children's
treasure chests.

Our treasure chests(orange and lemon boxes from
the grocery store, attractively covered with stick-on
paper) help the children cherish many moments to
remember. They contain their baby books—and what
a delight they are to us; a growing Book of Remembrance for each child; special letters and cards from

their uncle in the mission field; choice papers and art work; and anything that is of special significance. We are certain that school days and teenage activities, mission and college experiences will completely fill their treasure chests. Not only will these things stimulate wonderful memories, but we hope they will also encourage our children to look for and treasure the best in life always.

Evenings looking through our wedding book and other family records, viewing motion pictures and slides rank high on our list of the best in family fun.

We hope to perpetuate the tradition in our family of doing good unto others. The children love to work with Mother as she bakes and cooks. Then they can go together to take a loaf of bread or a pie or a cake to someone who is ill or needs cheering. How extra good our dinner tastes when the children know that some family with a newborn baby is enjoying a meal just like it. Refer to page 143 for lesson and ideas on sharing.

When kindnesses are expressed to one, it should be traditional—even in the life of a young child—to express appreciation personally or phone or write a special thank you. A thank you letter to Santa is a worthwhile project.

A weekly visit to the library or bookmobile to check out books is an event eagerly anticipated by children.

The far-reaching traditions of reading and praying together and going to church as a family cannot be overestimated in value. In fact, they are of such importance that entire sections of this book have been devoted to them.

As important and wonderful as is family togetherness, wise parents will take the time to enjoy each child individually, that no partiality is felt in the family. In large families or where several children are close together in age, children are sometimes lost in the shuffle and lack the personal attention they need. A parent should set aside some time for each child—even if it is only a half hour a week—and then do what *he* or *she* wants to do.

Perhaps time could be spent with one child while younger children are napping. Maybe your children could take turns staying up a half hour past bedtime for a special time with Mother and Daddy. Children might take turns accompanying Mother shopping. Dishwashing, ironing, hair setting provide times for visits.

What a treat it is to have Daddy take someone to the office with him, if he needs to be there for an hour or so some Saturday or holiday. An evening of fun when Daddy and daughter do something together, a few hours at the ball park with a father and son, or an overnight camping trip make for moments to remember.

A mother of five children says that, unknown to the children, she and her husband have agreed to devote one day a week to each child. During that day, one particular child is kept uppermost in the thoughts of the parents. They try to show him an extra amount of patience and understanding. They are alert to moments during the day when that child is alone, and they can join him for a visit or help him become interested in some activity. They put forth a special effort to help him or her with something in which he or she is especially interested, such as baking together, doing some sewing, or building with an erector set. The mother plans some of his or her favorite foods for the dinner and encourages the child to work with her in the meal preparation. Even though a good parent must be alert to every child's needs every day, it might avoid slighting one unintentionally to set up this type of system.

So often, making a moment to remember requires little extra time and effort—only some imagination. If we look at the routine happenings of the day with the idea of making some of them special, we can easily do it. One father, after being made aware of the importance of this, tells this story:

> Sunday has always been a special day at our house, but now it's extra special. After Sunday School and Sacrament meeting, we members of the bishopric remain in the foyer to speak with the members. I have made a schedule whereby each of my six daughters takes her turn to wait and walk home with me. Hand in hand we stroll along. We thrill to the beauty of the trees and flowers; we gaze at the twinkling stars and talk of all the wonderful things our Heavenly Father gives to us. Little personal problems often claim our conversation, too. Last week after Sunday School my four-year-old surprised me with the question, "Daddy, when we come alive again, will we be little babies?" I shall always cherish this opportunity to explain the resurrection to her in language she could understand. It was a precious experience for both of us. Believe me, I am looking for more such opportunities!
>
> —Making Moments to Remember
> *The Children's Friend*
> October 1962

Family projects and activities make some of the best moments to remember of all. Projects from raking the leaves or washing the car to a family "fix it night" when the mother and girls mend and the father and sons handle any maintenance work and repair job are fun as well as helpful. We have enjoyed family activities with our children such as taking them to visit a dairy, visiting the points in our city of religious and historical significance, having fun at the zoo and amusement parks, swimming, and picnicking. A family should make it a point to have a regular family activity.

A list of moments to remember could never be complete without the most important one of all— weekly family home evening.

Sometimes family home evenings are spontaneous —when families enjoy good times together without any advance planning. Actually family home evening—at least the spirit of family home evening—should be almost every evening.

You cannot force a child to do something or to become something; but as parents, it is your responsibility to provide the experience or situation that will help him most. If you hope to raise a choice family, you will have to provide them with choice experiences. A person truly does become the sum total of his experiences. Let us give our children a rich heritage of moments to remember.

CHURCH ATTENDANCE

PUZZLE PIECE VII

"If your family is to grow up in the church, your family must be in church."

One Sunday evening as Grandmother was getting ready for Sacrament meeting, her young grandson asked, "Grandmother, why do you still go to church each Sunday? You've been going for years and years and know all about the gospel. Why, no one could tell you anything new. You ought to stay home and rest once in a while."

The grandmother pointed to a bushel basket which was nearby and asked her grandson to take it to the creek and fill it with water. "Why, Grandmother," he said, "you know that basket can't hold any water." But the grandmother insisted, so the boy took the basket to the creek.

As he carried the basket back to his grandmother, the water seeped out all along the way until when he reached her there was only a little water left in the bottom. "See, Grandmother, the water is almost gone."

The grandmother replied, "This is just like going to church. Each week we are filled with the spirit of the gospel, but by the end of the week much of it has seeped out, and we need to be refilled. And besides, just as with the basket, in the process we are washed clean."

Children should grow up with the knowledge and understanding that the Lord has commanded us to attend Sacrament meeting, and that it is his desire that we should also attend Sunday School and other meetings held in his name. If we love the Lord, we will respond to his wishes as well as his commandments and will attend meetings. Parents and children need these meetings to renew covenants; we need these meetings to build us spiritually.

Wise parents will bring children up with the feeling (or attitude) that this commandment of church attendance is not a burden, but rather a blessing—in fact, numerous blessings of gospel knowledge, testimony strengthening experiences, closeness to the Lord, personal development, opportunities to serve, and all things which make possible a rich, spiritual life.

When children, as well as parents, attend church, they will *feel* the Spirit of the Lord there if they have an attitude of reverence and worship. Instead of going to church with the hope of finding the Spirit of the Lord there, we should take that spirit with us.

Mrs. Brown reported to the bishop that when her family returned home from Sacrament meeting Susie had said, "Oh, that was a boring meeting. I counted fifteen people who were asleep."

Eddie replied, "I wasn't bored. I bet you didn't see the airplanes on Mrs. Gilbert's dress. I thought at first they were just little lines. But they were planes going in all directions. So I drew airplanes."

Mrs. Brown suggested to the bishop that if children were expected to attend Sacrament meeting, it should be made more interesting for them.

The next day the bishop met Mrs. Peterson. She reported the reaction of her family to the same meeting. Linda had said, "I'm glad we sang 'I know That My Redeemer Lives.' That is my favorite hymn. It makes me tingle."

Tim remarked, "Mother, during the passing of the Sacrament, I thought of what you had said about Jesus dying to save us and that we had to do right to save ourselves. I remembered that lie I told last week, and I promised my Heavenly Father that I would watch myself this week and tell the truth, even if it meant I'd be punished for something I had done."

James added, "It's hard to be a good Christian. The speaker said that when someone hits you, you naturally want to hit him, but Jesus taught us to do him a kindness instead. Dad, do you think it would be all right to hit him first and then do him a kindness?"

The bishop had to conclude that the opposing reactions of the Brown family and the Peterson family reflected the attitude of the parents.

—Arta M. Hale
"Don't Close the Door"
The Children's Friend
April 1960

Members of the Church sometimes attend meetings with a negative attitude, depending upon the meeting to spiritually feed, edify and inspire them. In such instances, many of these people return home feeling disappointed and dissatisfied—even critical. Actually, the quality of the meeting depends upon each individual present.

A reverent congregation, beautiful music, and dynamic, stimulating speaking or teaching certainly contribute to the success and spirit of a meeting. But a meeting need not fail even in the absence of these conditions. The effectiveness of a meeting lies primarily in the heart of each member in attendance.

Parents should set an example for their children by going to church with an attitude of giving or contributing, not just getting or receiving. Theirs should be the spirit of service and love. They should radiate the gospel. They should join in the congregational singing with enthusiasm, and become united in spirit with those who pray. They should listen to every speech and lesson through ears of understanding and appreciation and make it a point to glean something of value on each occasion. They should glow with the spirit of friendliness and consider themselves on the welcoming committee to greet others, particularly strangers. There should be a prayer in their hearts for everyone participating. Then they will truly be spiritually fed and edified; the meeting will have been a source of inspiration to them.

If you want to feel the spirit of the Lord when you attend meetings, take it with you!

Let your children feel, as they grow up, that church is a meaningful and necessary part of your life. They will then be more inclined to accept it as a meaningful and necessary part of their own lives. Your example and attitude will do more to encourage their attendance at church than anything else you could ever do.

Even before children can comprehend the significance of church attendance and the message given there, they should go with you to church. This will help form a habit which they will carry through life.

A neighbor once gave this as the reason for his children's faithful attendance at church:

> We carry them when they are babies;
> We hold their hands when they are young;
> We walk beside them when they are grown.

Don't just send your children. *Go with them.* It is a blessed child who sees his parents in church every week.

Even a busy young mother, through good management, can attend Sunday School. Clothes can be readied earlier in the week and shoes can be polished on Saturday. Salads and desserts—as well as anything else for dinner—can be prepared on Saturday.

The mother might serve a "Continental Breakfast" every Sunday morning. This would mean the type of breakfast many European people eat: milk, juice, and sweet rolls. To further expedite getting to Sunday School, this breakfast could be served with paper cups and napkins. Eggnogs also provide quick, but nutritious breakfasts. Meats, prepared in a simple yet delicious way can be cooking in the oven while the family is at Sunday School.

On Sunday, housework should be kept to a minimum, such as just making beds and washing dishes.

Older children could help dress younger children. They could tie shoes, brush hair, button dresses. Other responsibilities, as well, should be delegated so that through teamwork everyone can be ready for Sunday School on time.

It is a father's responsibility and privilege to attend priesthood meeting with his sons and then join

with family members for other meetings. It should
be his policy that business affairs never interfere with
Sabbath day activities. This day should never be a
time for sports, washing the car, or yard work.

Wise parents would never ask a child if he wanted
to go to church. If each Sunday morning you considered the issue and tried to decide whether or not to go
to church, you would place yourself wide open for
the old adversary to work on you. There would be too
many opportunities to tempt you and cause you to
rationalize. Soon it would become so difficult to make
a decision that it would be much easier to stay home.
Actually there is no decision to make; early in life one
should determine to attend church every week. With
the exception of illness, *everyone* should be in church
every Sunday.

A mother of small children complained to her
mother, "I just can't see dragging the children across
the city to take them to church."

The grandmother replied, "Can't you, my dear?
I can think of women who were willing to drag their
children clear across the plains because of the gospel."

Teach your children church hymns in the home,
and then when they attend church, they will be able
to join in the congregational singing and will feel at
home.

Teach your children the gospel in the home, and
then when they attend meetings, they will be able to
better understand and learn from the speaker or teacher, and they will be able to answer questions intelligently in class. This will help them be more interested
in church; it will help them avoid embarrassment and
will help them feel that they belong in church.

Encourage your children to select friends from
their Sunday School class, Primary class, their MIA

group, their priesthood quorum or their seminary class.

Parents should not only help their children form wholesome attitudes toward church activity and develop positive habits for church attendance, but they should also provide a situation conducive to reverence and worship while they are with their family in the church building.

Children do need some special help in this regard. One little three-year-old boy said, "That's a long minute to have to sit still and listen to a bunch of stories."

It is helpful if you can plan to be in your seats about five minutes early and catch the mood as the organ prelude is played. A rush at the last minute is upsetting to both parents and children.

Make a point to sit in the front of the chapel so your children can *see* and *hear* easily.

The children's personal needs should be taken care of before entering the chapel so that they won't get into the very poor and unnecessary habit of leaving the meeting for drinks of water or going to the rest room.

Be where you are. Don't just attend church physically. Listen to what is being said. Listening, or not listening, is largely a habit. Get in the habit of listening!

Encourage your children to listen by having interesting discussions on the speakers' topics after the meeting. Don't be critical; just use the messages as a basis for a constructive gospel discussion.

From time to time have Family Hour lessons centered around reverence and proper behavior in a church building.

Don't reward naughtiness on the part of younger children by taking them out of a meeting and letting them run in the halls or yard. If children misbehave, they should find it more unpleasant to be taken out! With the exception of a bottle for the baby, it is best to leave toys and food home. After the Sacrament, however, a preschool child might have a pencil and one or two pieces of note paper to draw with.

Frequently remind children as you are preparing for church about the purpose and meaning of the Sabbath, the importance and significance of the Sacrament, and the reasons the Lord has commanded us to make all of this a part of our lives. Children will more willingly participate once they understand why.

Support and encourage your children's attendance in auxiliary organizations. Work with the auxiliaries in teaching your children.

One family who has several Primary-aged children, has developed an extensive picture file over a two or three year period. Each week after the children return home from Primary, they are allowed to go through the picture file and select one picture they feel illustrates best the lesson they heard that day. Each child then posts this picture in a plastic folder which stands on their dining room table. These pictures are left for the entire week as a reminder to the children of the things they learned. Of course, the picture idea is a wonderful incentive for children really to listen to the lessons, too.

Know your children's teachers and counsel with them and work with them in teaching your children.

Some parents became concerned about the swearing that their children and others in the neighborhood had suddenly picked up. The parents tried everything to stop it—they reasoned with the children, pleaded with them, punished them and prayed with them, but the bad language persisted. Finally, in desperation, the mother spoke to the Junior Sunday School co-ordinator about the problem. The co-ordinator invited the bishop to speak to the Junior Sunday School about language. Not another naughty word was uttered by the children.

It is a good idea to have Sunday dinner table discussion revolve around the class activities of each person. Encourage your children to explain what they learned in class and give them the opportunity to ask questions and clarify any point they don't fully understand. Take the time to satisfy their questions. Maybe the answer could be given in a special report by one family member on the next family night program.

Parents could also tell what they learned that day. This would help the children realize that parents are always learning, too; that the gospel is eternal in scope.

The social and recreational opportunities, as well as the gospel instruction, which the MIA offers provide an excellent medium for young people to grow spiritually, physically, mentally, and socially.

It seems that home training and church attendance form the foundation upon which a life of church activity and spirituality can be enjoyed. In this building of young lives, seminary attendance serves as a cornerstone. There, daily gospel lessons taught by capable, well-prepared teachers add greatly to one's gospel knowledge. A survey of students who graduated from seminary ten years ago was taken in the Southern California area. This survey revealed that 96% of all seminary students who graduated were married in the temple; 75% of the male graduates had fulfilled missions for the Church; 86% of the male graduates were active holders of the Melchizedek Priesthood.

The Lord, in his wisdom, has commanded us to attend church, to help us on our way to immortality and eternal life. As parents it is our responsibility to encourage this in our children. If your family is to grow up in the church, your family must be in church!

FAMILY GOALS

PUZZLE PIECE VIII

"If a man does not know to what port he is sailing, no wind is favorable to him."

"During the war, one morning," a GI recalled, "I was talking to a Sicilian peasant, and I asked him, 'Where does this road lead?'"

He thought for several minutes and then answered, "Well, Signore, if you go far enough, this road would take you to Rome. It would take you to Berlin. It would take you to London. It might even take you to Tokyo."

So it is with our goals in life.

This story brings three things to mind. We must first determine our goal. Will it be Berlin, London, or Tokyo? If we do not know where we are headed, we will most likely wander aimlessly about, wasting time on sideroads and never reach one of those places. Second, we must travel the right road in the right direction, or in other words, all our actions must lead toward the desired goal. Third, like this road, our goals will take us in any direction and as far as we desire.

No ship leaves a port, no train departs from a station, and no corporation goes into business without first determining the purpose and destination of the journey or business venture.

Marriage and parenthood, being ordained by God and eternal in purpose, should be entered into much more thoughtfully than any business venture.

President and Mrs. David A. Broadbent (former mission president and patriarch, and counselor in the Salt Lake Temple presidency before his death), made this plan early in their marriage:

Shortly after our marriage on May 1, 1901, in the Manti Temple, we prayerfully planned the following objectives for our family. First, we would welcome and prayerfully prepare for the coming of every child; second, we would have each child baptized on his eighth birthday, and we would give him an account book for his individual record of all receipts and disbursements chiefly for the purpose of training him in thrift and industry, and so that he would fully observe the law of tithing; third, we would keep each child busy in all home and farm duties according to his age and train him for full participation in all church and civic activities, and to keep before him the best in church and other literature; fourth, we would assist each child to secure a college education if he was academically inclined, or if not, assist him in vocational training so that he could earn a living and be financially independent of government or church relief; fifth, we would strive to have all the boys fill missions for the Church, and we would encourage and assist all the girls who might be called to serve as missionaries; and, sixth, we would endeavor to instil in every child a desire to be married in the temple.

Years of labor and love went into the accomplishment of their ideals. They had twelve children. Their aspirations were realized.

"Many of our neighbors, who have had double the income and half the number of children, have wondered, 'Where is their pot of gold? We have not been able to send our children on missions or to college. How do they do it?'"

"The answer is plain," says President Broadbent. "Where there is no vision, the family perishes. Get an aim. Formulate a plan, and then work your plan co-operatively. We have often wished that our income might have been double what it was, but today, we say, unreservedly, 'Thank God we have never been cursed with either poverty or with riches.' Each one has been privileged to exert and assert his full power in bringing out the native talents and abilities God has blessed him with."

"A Forty-five Year Mission in Prepared Parenthood"
An Interview with David A. and Mima Murdock Broadbent
The Improvement Era, August 1946.

The Broadbents' Plan represents the ideal way to begin a marriage. It would be wise even for engaged couples to outline such a plan to make certain their values in life and their desires and dreams coincide. "True love does not consist in gazing at each other but in looking forward together in the same direction."

As children grow, they should become increasingly aware of their family goals. Sometimes children get the feeling that getting the new car paid for, completing the landscaping, or meriting that job promotion are our only important goals because we talk about them so much. As parents, we must place emphasis on spiritual goals and make certain our children understand these. Sometimes parents have ideals and plans for their children, but they neglect to tell the children about them. It is sad to hear a young LDS boy say, "I have never thought much about going on a mission," or to hear a lovely girl say, "I haven't given temple marriage much thought."

Parents should stimulate their children toward thinking about these things from childhood, and the family should consciously and actively work toward reaching the goals they have set up. They should periodically evaluate their lives to make sure they are headed in the right direction.

Teach children to plan for the future. "It is recommended that we take an interest in the future—that's where we'll spend the rest of our lives."

Keep goals constantly before your children and help them to weigh all their activities to see if they are in accordance with these goals. "Where you go hereafter depends upon what you go after here."

A "This Is Your Life" chart would be an excellent thing to present to each child, perhaps illustrated and framed. "Ideals are like stars—like the mariners on the sea we chart our course by them." See pages 86 and 87.

The privilege of having a patriarchal blessing has been given to the members of the Church. As parents, we should help our children understand and appreciate such a blessing and gain the desire to have one. This blessing, given through inspiration, can assist a young person greatly in charting his course in life. It gives him blessings for which to live, and can be a guide, incentive, and comfort in his life.

THIS IS YOUR LIFE
(for girls)

Age	Mission Fund	Church Activity	Educational Plan	Social Life
8		Baptism	Grammar School	Boys can't play
9		Primary and		hopscotch and
10		Sunday School		jump-the-rope
11				nearly as well as girls!
12		M I A (with a goal to	Junior	
13		earn an individaul	High	
14		award and class award)	School	Group-type
		Seminary		Social
15		Continued	High	Activities
16		activity in MIA, Sunday School,	School	First Date
17		Sacrament Meeting, Seminary and	College, work, or mission	
18		Institute Regular Church	To help me reach my life-long ambition.	Selective
19		Attendance	Whichever I choose	Dating and Courtship
20		Officer or Teacher in one of the	I know it must be the best to pre-pare me for my	Leading
21		Auxiliary Organiza-tions	own family. Being a wife and a mother	Toward Temple Marriage
22		Temple Marriage and commence-	is a glorious duty. I must prepare myself humbly	
23		ment of parent-hood	for my role in eternity.	

"Seek ye first the kingdom of God, and all else shall be added unto you."

THIS IS YOUR LIFE
(for boys)

Age	Mission Fund	Church Activity	Educational Plan	Social Life
8		Baptism	Grammar School	
9		Cub Scouts, Continue		Girls ? ?
10		Primary and Sunday School		What are
11		Become a full-		They? ! ?
12		fledged Scout	Junior	
13		Receive Aaronic Priesthood, ordained	High School	
14		a deacon		
15		Ordained a teacher	High	Group-type Social Activities.
16		Commence seminary program.	School	Friendly, individual
17		Ordained a priest		and double dating. Limited use of
18		Enroll in Institute Program	Freshman at College	family car.
19		Ordained Elder in Melchizedek		Selective dating and
20		Priesthood— Mission call		courtship period leading
21		Release from honorable mission	Sophomore at College	toward a Temple Marriage
22		Temple Marriage and commence-	Junior at College	
23		ment of parent- hood	Graduate from College	

"Seek ye first the kingdom of God, and all else shall be added unto you."

Let's first discuss *material* goals. The Savior told us: "Seek ye first the kingdom of God, and all else shall be added unto you."

It is not money, but the love of money, that is the root of all evil. The Lord wants his people to prosper—that is one purpose for the law of tithing—but not just so we can heap up the things of the world. The Lord wants us to be blessed materially so that we can develop ourselves educationally and culturally, so we can better help our fellow men and so we can serve him.

Every family desires to have the means to live comfortably. We are better able to keep spiritual laws if our physical needs have been satisfied. It is a blessed family where the father is a good provider and where a reasonable amount of physical security is enjoyed.

Some families, however, feel that they *need everything* money can buy. Then the acquisition of material things becomes an overpowering goal, and their values become distorted, and spiritual matters become neglected. Maybe a father holds down two jobs just to bring home things which really aren't that important and consequently fails to spend time enough with his children or doesn't have the time to be active in the Church. Sometimes a mother turns her home and family over to someone else's care and gets a job, when it really isn't necessary. Children need a mother at home much more than they need the things extra money can buy.

Families sometimes over-extend themselves financially and then bills and creditors consume too much thought and effort. It's difficult to have fun with your children and take time to serve in the Church when money worries plague you.

A family should budget their money so that some of it is allocated to cultural and educational pursuits. Invest some money in things you can take with you—memories and experiences gleaned from travel, theatrical productions, symphonies, concerts, adult education classes, music, and other lessons.

A wealthy man was killed in a highway automobile accident. From the crowd of people who gathered at the scene of the accident, some asked: "I wonder how much money he left behind?"

Someone else answered, "All of it."

*   *   *

An ideal family will have *educational* goals. We know that the "Glory of God is intelligence." (D&C 93:36.) We have also been told by the Lord: "Whatever principle of intelligence we attain unto in this life, it will rise with us in the resurrection." (*Ibid.*, 130:18.)

It is a worthy desire of every parent to help children grow up with a quest for knowledge, a love of good books, and a compelling desire to gain the training and skill to succeed in life.

This is an age of specialization. A young person must be well qualified—either through academic or vocational training—in order to make his contribution toward society. Today a farmer can farm better if he has had agricultural training. A laborer can do well if he is skilled and trained. Specialized training is the door to the professions. A young girl who learns homemaking skills—and who also develops herself in other ways—will enjoy a rich, rewarding life as a homemaker.

A parent can do much to encourage a child toward educational goals by creating an atmosphere of learning and inquiry in the home. Samuel Langley said, "Knowledge begins with wondering. Set a child to wondering and you have put him on the road to understanding."

Children should grow up with bedtime stories and picture books. Good books for all ages should be available. Family reading projects, as mentioned previously, can promote good reading in the family.

Television can also contribute towards a child's education *if it is controlled.* Selected, choice programs can be very beneficial and do much to enrich a child's life; a diet of too much television can dull a child's ability to use his own resources; it can pollute his mind with trash; it can cause him to be mentally and physically lazy.

The solution to the television challenge is not to keep it out of the house but to learn to use it right. A parent should work with a child in the selection of programs so that his ability to discern is developed. Television, like atomic energy, can be used to either build us up or destroy us. Wise families will use it for the blessing it can be.

Music appreciation is a vital part of a child's education. Children can gain a love for music if good music is played in the home and occasional concerts and symphonies are attended. Many metropolitan areas present special concerts for the youth. An occasional dinner table discussion or Family Hour Program could be centered around the life and works of a composer. (Information and pictures from the life of a great composer and recordings of his music can be obtained from the library.) Music lessons further help children gain an appreciation and understanding of music.

A culture-minded mother says that her children are learning to enjoy art just through being exposed to it. She checks out copies from the masters at the library and posts one weekly in the home. As her children ask questions about the painting, she has many "Teaching Moments" to help them appreciate it as well as the artist. A recent trip to the art gallery proved to be a delightful event for her children as they recognized many familiar paintings.

A wholesome attitude toward school and teachers should prevail. A poor attitude on the part of parents can tear down all that they are trying to build up.

A mother complained that her little boy wasn't learning to read as he should. Then she added, in his presence, "But I'm not surprised; I think the schools today are terrible."

Our little children had talked of going to college some day until one afternoon a baby sitter told them that she didn't want to go to college because it was too much work.

Fortunately this baby sitter's influence was only momentary. There will be many years for us to help our children realize that college is work, that it is a challenge, but that the rewards are numerous. We want them to feel that work is the price we pay for success, that challenges build us as people and are the steppingstones leading toward goals.

* * *

Spiritual goals are the most significant of all. Let's consider them on an immediate, a future, and an eternal basis.

An ideal family is immediately concerned with matters leading toward the goals of obedience, discipline, wholesome attitudes, high morals, worthwhile values, and positive character traits.

As a young man, Benjamin Franklin felt there were some character traits which he would like to make part of his personality. He listed these traits—temperance, order, industry, and so on—on thirteen different cards. He kept these cards in his coat pocket and each week he concentrated on the top card and made a conscious effort to have that particular virtue become a part of him. At the end of the week he would put the top card on the bottom and work on the next card. Benjamin Franklin repeated this thirteen card process throughout his life. Today these qualities and virtues are the things we most admire about him.

Benjamin Franklin's thirteen step program could be of value to our families. Parents could guide their children in selecting several qualities, listing them on cards, and then working on them one at a time, a week at a time. (It would be well for parents to have a similar project for themselves. "The day parents begin to work on their own problems, the child can only improve.")

A lovely young mother applies this same character-developing principle in the lives of her very young children. Each week she posts a word—such as love, obey, happiness, honesty, kindness—in a special spot in the kitchen. That word becomes the family theme for the week and everyone puts forth special effort to make it part of his life. The mother says her children remind other brothers and sisters about this matter. One week a little boy failed to mind. His older brother said, "The word is *obey*. That's O-B-E-Y." This is helping their spelling, too!

One family posts a scripture on the bathroom mirror each week, and by the end of the week everyone in the family knows it. Things which are learned young in life, stay with a person.

A mother of ten fine children says that in her family, achievement has been encouraged and recognized by converting a lovely antique frame into a special display area for their children's pins and medals. Her children have all been active in 4-H Club, scouting, school, and Church, and the many pins and medals they earned were becoming misplaced and forgotten until they thought of the frame idea. The black velvet lining of the frame sets the pins off well and each child's name in miniature gold letters marks his particular collection. As well as being an attractive wallpiece, this serves further to encourage her children to excel and gives the younger members of the family something for which to strive.

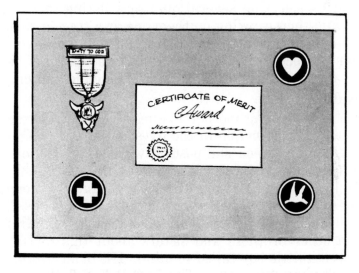

A variation of this idea could be small individual frames (perhaps oval shaped) for each child's pins. These could be arranged in an attractive grouping on a wall.

Of course, parents and children will understand that the pin or medal is only a symbol. The important thing is the growth and development which takes place in the life of the person who earned the recognition. Children should be guided in doing the right thing for the right reason.

Where there is no vision, a family perishes. Have dreams—visions—for the future. Work to make these dreams come true.

Don't just hope that your little sons will someday grow up to be missionaries. Help them to *want* to go because they have a testimony of the gospel and feel a strong desire to share this with others so that they, too, might enjoy the blessings which the gospel can bring. As you pray with them, ask the Lord to bless them so that someday they will grow up to be good missionaries. Don't say "If you go . . ." but rather, "When you go . . ." Give them a savings bank for mission money. LDS bookstores sell a special bank which is divided into three partitions: one section for tithing, the center section for mission, and the third section for spending money. A little boy who puts away pennies for a mission will be more inclined to live for a mission. As a boy grows older and has a job, he should be guided in saving part of that money for his mission. One mother bakes two batches of bread each week. One is for her family, and the other batch is for her nine-year-old boy to sell to their neighbors. This brings him $1.80 a week. He is putting aside part of that money for a mission fund. It is not just that the money will be helpful in keeping him on a mission; it is that the money might get him there in the first place!

The Bancroft Ward of Idaho claims a notable achievement in missionary work. Of the 550 members of the ward, 19 are serving as missionaries.

Planning for this achievement began quite some years back under the leadership of Bishop Glenn F. Yost. A world map on the ward bulletin board has a bright thread strung from a picture of the missionary to the spot on the map where each is laboring.

But Bishop Yost begins early. For example, to George Millward, just ordained to the office of deacon, the bishop recently handed a small world globe with this note:

"Dear George: Some day the President of the LDS Church will no doubt call you to go to some part of the world as a missionary. Start today to prepare yourself, physically, spiritually, and financially for a mission. May this little bank, and the coins dropped in, encourage you towards starting a growing savings account, that you will be prepared when the call comes. Encouragingly, Bishop Yost."

That's how all 19 missionaries got their start and a score or more of deacons, teachers, and priests are now working toward the same objective.

—The Church News Section
The Deseret News

A boy shouldn't wait until he is nineteen to start preparing for a mission. He should also prepare himself through gospel study. Studying a foreign language can be very useful. Even if he is never called to a land where he can use that particular language, just the fact that he has studied a language will aid him in learning another language faster and easier.

Children often love to look through their parents' wedding album and are eager to hear the explanation of each thing that took place. They are delighted with the pictures but find it takes a little time to realize why they, too, are not in the picture! Each time our family passes the temple, one of the children exclaims, "Oh, there's where Mother and Daddy were married." Then often, as they play house, they pretend that someone is getting married. It thrills us as parents to see them don white dress-up

clothes for the make-believe occasion and go to the
"temple" for this special event. They are growing up
with the idea that marriage and temple are synonymous. We hope by the time they learn that it isn't
always so, a foundation will have been laid so they
will still feel that in their lives the two must go together.

An LDS girl who is truly anticipating temple
marriage will not invest in sleeveless or low-backed
clothes during the teenage years, so that her wardrobe
will be unsuited for the modest type of clothing a
temple marriage requires.

Young people who are looking forward to temple
marriage must also have a "temple courtship"—that
is, they must date only people who uphold the gospel
standards and who are worthy of a temple marriage
and who desire to be married in the temple.

A family's dreams and goals should lead them
right into eternity. Eternal glory and perfection are
a process, not an event. The kingdom of God—unlike
kingdoms of this world—requires a person to live its
laws in advance. We must live celestial laws *now* if
we expect to live them hereafter. If we want to have
our family in heaven, we must have heaven in our
family.

The perpetuation of family life throughout all
eternity is the greatest of all blessings. Parents and
children who truly understand the gospel—who know
"why"—would not let one little earthly thing stand in
their way of gaining this.

The importance of family goals is expressed in
the song, "Happy Talk," from *South Pacific:* "You've
got to have a dream. If you don't have a dream, how're
you going to have a dream come true?"

SYSTEMATIC
TEACHING

Puzzle Piece IX

> I saw tomorrow marching by
> On little children's feet;
> Within their forms and faces read
> Her prophecy complete.
>
> I saw tomorrow look at me
> From little children's eyes,
> And thought how carefully we'd teach
> If we were really wise!
> —Walt Whitman

A traveler visited a church in Germany, famous for its stained-glass windows. The exterior was plain and there was no beauty in the windows from outside—there never is, you know.

As the traveler stepped inside, he felt a keen disappointment. It was drab and dark and uninviting. A very old guide directed him forward and, looking to the east where the sun was shining, a marvelous sight broke upon him. There was Jesus in the temple with the doctors. The guide urged him to return at noon. He then found another window in the sun, and Jesus was walking upon the water.

The old guide begged him to return one last time at sunset. These rays fell upon Christ on the cross.

Through the careful insistence of the guide, the traveler saw the choice views in the church, but many other visitors had come to the church and found disillusionment. Some viewed only the outside; others looked at the windows from the wrong angle; and still other came on a foggy day. No one directed them.

(Author unknown.)

It is much the same with the youth of the Church. Before them stands a priceless treasure, but without guidance and direction they cannot see the beauty of it.

If parents fail to give their children an understanding of the gospel principles, it is possible that they, like many travelers to the old German church, will find only disillusionment and turn away in disappointment. The responsibility lies in the home.

If every baby who is born came equipped with a set of instructions pasted on his back about how to handle him and teach him, it would be a cinch to guide him effectively. Or if there were a list published for parents of all the questions a child would need to know and another list of all the answers, success would be so easy to attain. But we cannot give our children all the answers. All we can do is effectively and systematically teach them, to give them a little light that they might see better.

In the Doctrine and Covenants 29:47 it tells us that power is not given to Satan to tempt little children until they have reached the age of accountability. Realizing this, we know it is so important for them to be taught the gospel during their young, impressionable years. We cannot leave the teaching to chance —it must be well-planned, and must be of the character-building, faith-promoting, testimony-giving kind.

Have you ever spent more time ironing out the wrinkles you've ironed in a shirt than it would have taken to have done it right to begin with? So it is with teaching children the gospel. We must start right with infancy and *be consistent over the years* if we don't want to spend later years ironing out the mistakes.

The Lord has commanded parents to bring up their children in light and truth. (D&C 93:40.) If they do not, the sin will be upon the parents' heads. (*Ibid.*, 68:25.) Even though we do teach our children to live and love the gospel, this is no guarantee that they all will. Certainly the chances of their being faithful are better, however, and at least the parents will have done their best to live up to the trust the Lord has given them in guiding his children, and they won't be held accountable for their children's actions in life.

Sometimes children, as they become older, grow away from the Church and what in life is precious and important. But parents must never, never give them up as lost. They must still try to influence them through love and example, faith and prayers. It is never too late.

Extremes in anything are undesirable. Just as it is wrong to leave the teaching of your children to chance, it is wrong to go overboard and give them too much too fast. Don't push them so hard to get everything that they want nothing. Every lesson must be taught with love. Moderation in all things should be the guide. Parents must also join their children in wholesome good times, creative projects and cultural activities. Actually, this is all part of the gospel because the Lord wants us to live a balanced life, and seek after all things which are of good report or praiseworthy.

In teaching children the gospel, help them to see the "why" of it. Young people who truly understand that their bodies are temples of God and are to be prepared for a glorious resurrection, don't defile them by taking into them impurities. Young people who truly understand that creation is in partnership with God do not misuse this great law. Young people who can see the significance of the ordinances of baptism, confirmation, and temple work remain true to those covenants. Young people who love the Lord keep his commandments.

A young person's reasons for keeping any commandment should be based on his obedience to the first two commandments: "Thou shalt love the Lord thy God with all thy heart and thy neighbour as thyself." It is of little value to keep a secondary law without first adhering to the primary law. A little boy was watching a television show in which the hero swaggered into the barroom and shot and killed his rival. The little boy's mother was horrified that her child should be watching such a program. Her son reassured her by saying: "It's okay, Mommy. He didn't drink anything."

If parents were asked to list their possessions in order of importance, their children would probably head the list. If asked, "What do you want most for your children?" any true Latter-day Saint parent would reply: "A testimony of the gospel and activity in the Church." Yet few parents give much consistent thought as to how this is going to be brought about. We sometimes feel that because we have a testimony, our children will automatically acquire one. President Grant used to say that both he and his wife knew the multiplication tables extremely well, yet none of their children were born with this skill. They all had to learn the multiplication tables for themselves. That same principle applies to getting a testimony.

Investigators in the mission field gain strong testimonies and knowledge of the gospel through missionaries who teach by the spirit and in a systematic way. In our homes are some little investigators who need to be taught the gospel by the spirit—by parents who love the gospel and who are close to the Lord; and in a systematic way—not in just a hit and miss fashion, allowing chance to play too big a part.

Do not neglect to answer questions on the spot. Teaching moments are priceless. Just be certain that you are teaching by having "planned moments" as well.

To teach the gospel effectively to their children, parents must understand, live and love the gospel. In other words, they must *have a testimony.*

A person soon learns how little he knows when a child begins to ask questions. A little girl asked her father, "What is a millennium?" The father answered, "Ah . . . well . . . you see, a millennium is like a centipede, only it has more legs!"

If you do not know the answer, admit it, but promise to find out. If a question is important enough to ask, it is important enough for an answer.

"There are two kinds of knowing things; you know something, or you know where you can find out about it. The one is no less important than the other."

Many parents feel that their knowledge of the gospel is inadequate, and they hesitate to teach their children. Instead of ignoring this responsibility, parents should let their children's questions lead them into studying the gospel and developing stronger testimonies. They will set up a systematic plan of study for their own development. They will assign themselves a subject each week to learn about.

We have already discussed the importance of example. To teach the gospel, parents must live the gospel. Also, to teach the gospel, the parents' love for it must radiate in their lives.

Their testimony of the gospel must be felt by the children. Parents should bear their testimonies both at church and at home so their children can hear them. Their love and respect for the gospel should be reflected in all they do.

Wise parents will prepare to teach the gospel to their children just as they would prepare to teach the gospel in a Sunday School class. (When you are to present a lesson to a Primary or Sunday School class, practise it on your children. They enjoy "helping" you and everyone gains. It is valuable for both you and them.) First of all, they will collect material such as visual materials, stories, examples, and songs. Once parents catch the spirit of collecting and filing, it can become a most fun as well as profitable hobby.

Second, wise parents will take the time to prepare lessons for their children. They will work with a PHD: prayerfully, humbly, and diligently.

Parents must never put off teaching because they feel they are too busy this week. Parents are busy every week, and if they wait until they have the time, that time will never come. People find the time to do whatever they enjoy and think is important. What could be more enjoyable and important than sharing your testimony and knowledge of the gospel with your children? The results and satisfaction will be so rewarding, that you will *want* to take the time. You will feel much like the Chinese philosopher who was asked what his happiest moment had been. He replied, "It was when I heard a child go singing along the pathway after he had asked me the way."

Each time you are tempted to put off this teaching program, ask yourself these two questions regarding your child's gospel education:

> *If not now, when?*
> *If not be me, by whom?*

Present these lessons for family home evenings or on other occasions. Plan the time, work for the time, and then take the time. These presentations should be pleasant and informal, but you will have to have the same discipline and attention from your children as you would from a Sunday School class. Help them feel the importance of this. Supplementary stories and lessons for teaching the gospel in the home can be found on pages 109 to 220.

The lessons should meet the needs and interests of the children. A series of lessons before a child's eighth birthday should prepare him for baptism. A young boy should be taught about the history, significance, and responsibility of the priesthood before he is ordained a deacon. A timely lesson on honesty could do much to help a child resist temptation.

Sometimes an older child could prepare, with the assistance and guidance of the parents, the lessons to be given younger children. A teenager could gain a great deal from teaching a young sister or brother the importance of baptism. A son who has been ordained a priest or an elder will help himself by helping a young brother understand the purpose and responsibility of the priesthood.

When a child asks questions regarding certain areas of the gospel, prepare a lesson answering these questions and present it immediately, even though you may have planned to give that particular lesson a little later.

The lessons should be challenging and should be developed to the age level of the children.

> Two first-graders were about to enter the school when a huge jet flew over. "That's a BX-50," said one.
>
> "No, it isn't—it's a BX-41," said the other, "and it's not going more than 750 miles an hour because it didn't break the sound barrier."
>
> The first boy agreed as to the speed, and said: "It's really amazing the pressure that develops on those planes when they go into a dive—almost 1,200 pounds per square inch."
>
> Just then the school bell rang, and the first boy sighed and said: "Oh, well, let's go in and string those darned beads again."

Our lessons must be challenging to children, but at the same time they must be developed and presented to their age level.

> He who would truly lead children,
> Be he ever so strong and wise,
> Must bring himself back to childhood
> And see things through children's eyes.

Jacob Hamblin was successful in his dealings with the Indians because he had the ability to reason with the Indians as an Indian.

There was a worker in the steel mills in Chicago who, in his spare time, had earned a graduate degree in psychology. He had given his thesis the title, "Why the Foreman Hates the Boss." His graduate committee changed it to read, "Emotional Coefficient Correlative in Inter-Personal Relation between Management and Supervising Echelons."

Matthew Cowley said, "The gospel is simply beautiful and beautifully simple." That is the way it must be taught to children.

However, our teaching methods must develop as a child develops and keep pace with his understanding. A lesson that is challenging to an eight-year-old will seem dull and silly to a teenager. The lesson must progress with the intellectual maturity of a child so he won't ever reach a point where they seem childish and foolish.

A brilliant young member of the Church announced his plans to study for a doctor's degree in philosophy. Some of his friends and family members foresaw the loss of his testimony and his falling away from the Church. He assured them this would not happen and stated his plans to study the gospel right along with philosophy, which he did.

During the years of his graduate work, he also completed an extensive study of the Doctrine and Covenants. As he was graduated with a PhD, he also had a stronger testimony than ever of the divinity of the Church and the truthfulness of the gospel. He is a great spiritual leader and among other assignments has served the Church well as a mission president.

Some people get a doctor's degree from a university but have only a third grade understanding of the gospel. Gospel study and knowledge must keep pace with academic study and knowledge.

As has been pointed out, teaching your children the gospel effectively will take time, effort, and study. But if you really *want* to, you will find the time by planning for it, working for it and taking it, and will put forth the necessary effort and study.

> To have sown in the souls of men
> One thought that will not die—
> To have been a link in the chain of life
> Shall be immortality.

A rancher drove his pickup truck across a frozen reservoir one day last winter. The ice broke, and the truck plunged into eleven feet of water. The rancher tried to open the door but couldn't. Finally, with water almost up to his head, Murphy, the rancher, broke the truck window and forced his body through. He came up under the ice.

He held his breath, opened his eyes and swam until he found the hole made by the truck.

He came up gasping for air, but he had nothing to grip to allow him to climb onto the ice from the frigid water of the reservoir. The forty-four-year-old rancher laid his arms on the ice and waited until his gloves and sleeves froze to the surface. Then he hauled himself out.

The rancher was alone, seven miles from camp. His wet clothing froze to ice in minutes in the eight degrees below zero temperature.

He set out and walked the seven miles, his frozen clothing cracking with every step. Finally, he staggered into his cabin, built a fire in the oil stove, waited until he was warmed, then set out on horseback to a home of a friend, three miles away.

What was this rancher fighting for? He was fighting for life. Because of this he performed a near impossible feat.

As mothers and fathers, we are also fighting for life. We're fighting for the happy, successful lives of our children. We're fighting for their eternal lives. No effort could be too great to make this life possible.

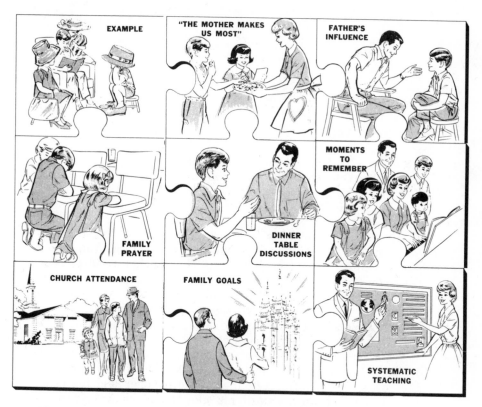

The pieces of a puzzle when standing all alone
Have little of the beauty that together may be shown.
Though the message of the puzzle may inspired be
One puzzle piece alone is not enough, you see.

And even if the puzzle is missing just one piece,
The value of the puzzle will surely decrease.
For a partial picture puzzle brings so little pleasure,
While a puzzle all completed is a thing that one can treasure.

The puzzle pieces of teaching are like this, for they should
Be entirely complete to be fully understood.
And if just one piece is missing, the child may not know
What a glorious thing he has that might set his heart aglow.

So, parents, give your children a testimony strong;
Give them knowledge and the wisdom to know the right from
    wrong;
Give them love and understanding; give them all the help
    they need
To understand the gospel—then its message they will heed!

Supplementary Stories, Activities and Lessons for Teaching the Gospel in the Home

Retold Stories

The story is told of a great king and queen who lived long, long ago. One day a little prince was born to them, and the king gave a special feast and invited all the people of his kingdom to come so that they might rejoice together.

The great and wealthy men brought costly gifts to the little babe, with the exception of one young and very wise man. He came empty handed. However, he said to the king, "Your son has received many costly gifts. I will give him something more precious than jewels and gold. Each day as he grows I will tell him a story that will make him wise and righteous."

Each day as the years went by this young man came to the palace. Each day he told the little boy a story. The child did become wise and righteous because what he learned through the stories helped determine the kind of man he became.

We parents have a gift to give our children which is more precious than jewels and gold. The greatest gift we can give them is that of *teaching them how to live, teaching them to love and obey the Lord, and instilling in their hearts a testimony of the gospel of Jesus Christ.*

A retold story is often much more effective in influencing children (grown-ups too, for that matter) than generalizing, preaching, or lecturing. The greatest teacher of all, Jesus Christ, taught his people through stories, using the terminology and illustrations which were familiar to them. These parables are classic examples of excellent teaching.

Good stories, well told, are a vital part of successful family home evenings.

The many choice, well-developed stories in the *Church Family Home Evening Manual* offer a wonderful aid to us in teaching our children. Wise, conscientious parents are constantly alert to story ideas from other sources, too, which can meet various needs with their children and help these children grow up to be wise and righteous.

BUILD CHARACTER

An edifying story can help to build children's characters and make them better people. Strength in overcoming weaknesses and faults can be gained through stories, as you can see in this one adapted from the one our grandmother told us as children:

Gertie the Grumbler

Gertie was a lovely little girl who had pretty dark curls and blue eyes. She was learning to play the piano well, and she was a good student at school. Gertie was lovely, except for one terrible habit. She was a groaner and complainer. No matter what happened or what she did, there was always some reason why Gertie couldn't be happy or pleased. It seemed to her family that she grumbled constantly. That's why her mother and father and older brother called her Gertie the Grumbler.

The time came that Gertie was to turn nine years old. In an attempt to make Gertie happy, her mother had told her she could have a birthday party. It was Gertie's privilege to invite just as many friends as she wanted. She also chose the games and activities, the flavor of ice cream, and the decorations for the cake. Her parents even let her select a new dress to wear to the party. Everything was done to please Gertie and make her happy.

Gertie's young friends had a delightful time at the party. It had been a grand success—at least so Gertie's parents thought. But when it was over, Gertie wasn't happy. She was sorry she had invited Ann. If she had invited Betty instead, Betty might have given her the pen and pencil set. Ann's gift was a book she had already read. Gertie complained about her own decision of having chosen to take her friends to the zoo instead of a show. How she wished they had gone to the matinee instead. She grumbled about the refreshments. Strawberry ice cream is so common; she should have chosen the peppermint after all. Her new dress didn't suit her, she said. She wished she had taken the blue sailor style rather than this one.

That's how it always was. No matter what Gertie's family, friends, and teachers did to make her happy, Gertie found a reason to grumble. It wasn't long before Gertie didn't have any friends. Her teachers would shake their heads and say, "Gertie could be such a lovely, sweet girl if she just didn't grumble so much." Gertie's parents tried and tried to help her see this problem, but Gertie went right on grumbling.

A few years later when Gertie was a teenager, her older brother went away to school. Gertie loved her brother very much and decided to prepare a special box to send him for his birthday. She spent days baking his favorite cookies and wrapping them to be mailed. She took the baby-sitting money she had earned the past few weeks and bought him a beautiful sport sweater— the kind he said he would like to have. There was even enough money left over to buy him a pair of socks to match the sweater. She included two magazines he liked to read as an extra surprise. After the box was mailed, she could hardly wait to receive his thank-you letter. She waited and waited, but no letter came.

When her brother returned home for Christmas vacation, Gertie asked first thing about the birthday box she had sent. "Oh," he said, "I got it all right, but by the time I shared the cookies with my roommates there weren't many left for me. I wish the sweater had been green instead of blue. That's the color all the fellows are wearing this season. And the next time you send me something, remember I like stretch socks better than the ones you bought. The dormitory lounge is full of reading material if I should ever have any time after studying, so don't bother about magazines any more."

By this time Gertie was in tears. How could her brother be so ungrateful, so unappreciative of all she had done? How could he be such a grumbler and complainer? Then Gertie saw it all. Her brother was merely treating her as she had treated him and everyone else all her life. Suddenly she realized what a terrible grumbler she had been. She had let the bad habit of complaining and finding fault with things take over her life and spoil her personality.

The day her brother taught her this valuable lesson marked the turning point in Gertie's life. From that time on she looked for the best in everything that happened. It was really hard at first. Grumbling had become such a habit with Gertie that she found herself grumbling without even realizing it. Each time she caught herself even thinking about it, she would try harder to put a happy thought in her mind in its place. It became her dream to become known as Gertie the Gracious One or Gertie the Grateful One. And before long she was!

MOVE TO LAUGHTER OR TEARS

Stories can inspire and touch children emotionally and cause them to respond with more grateful hearts, more generous natures, and a rededication to things in life which are most precious and important.

Joey

The store windows were just as magnificent as they had been last week, but Joey stared unseeingly into them. He didn't notice the electric train that he had admired for over a half hour just a few days ago; and he didn't laugh when the toy conductor hopped on and off at each station. Joey was thinking about last night.

In all his nine years, he had never had to make such an important decision. When he had come home from school, he noticed that his mother, who was usually cheerful, looked worried. After dinner, Joey's mother had said, "Joey, you help Connie get to bed, will you, please?"

"Of course," Joey had replied. "What story are you going to read us tonight?"

"None, tonight dear," his mother had said, and Joey was too surprised to protest. He could not remember one single night that his mother had not read them a story or poem. Connie had gone quietly to bed because she, too, was confused. After Joey had listened to his little sister's simple prayer, he returned to the kitchen.

"Joey," his mother said then, "I want to talk to you." They both sat down at the kitchen table. "It's about Rags. Rags is a good little dog and never causes

any trouble at all, but it still costs money to feed him."
Joey kept his eyes down. He was afraid of what was
coming. "You need a new winter coat badly this year,
and yesterday when I priced them they were more expensive than I had counted on. I'm sorry, Joey, but if
we keep Rags, you can't have a winter coat this year."

Joey knew that he needed the winter coat. His old
one was so terribly small it looked silly on him and was
so worn out and torn that it didn't begin to keep the
cold out. But Joey also needed Rags. He looked at the
little dog lying by the cold hearth. Connie played with
the dog all day while Joey was at school. What would
she do without Rags? But, what would he do without a
winter coat? His mother continued. "I love Rags as
much as you do, Joey. The decision is yours."

Joey thought. "Can I tell you in the morning?"

"Of course," his mother had said. Joey knew that
his mother realized how he loved the little dog he had
found three years ago. She gave him a hug and a kiss,
and he had run off to bed. But he did not sleep. He had
cried and cried all night long because he knew what
the decision must be. His eyes were red and swollen
when he told his mother that he would take Rags to
town after school and give him away to somebody. His
mother had tried to smile. "Some other family can
probably give him better food and a warmer place to
sleep than we can anyway." Joey knew this was true.

A sudden bark reminded Joey that he was down-
town with Rags in his arms. He had been there an hour
and his feet and hands were ice-cold. He gave Rags a
squeeze and touched his lips to Rags' ear. He started
slowly up the street. People couldn't help noticing the
tiny figure who was so thinly clad and carrying a dog.
Nor could they overlook the expression of complete un-
happiness that was on his face. While passing the pet
store Joey heard a little boy say, "Oh, Mother, I'm go-

ing to ask Santa to bring me that little spotted puppy,"
Joey looked at the little boy. Then he looked at the lady
beside him as she said, "But, Richard, Santa is already
bringing you so many things that he hasn't room in his
bag for a puppy dog." Joey took a deep breath and
walked up to the boy. "You can have this dog. His
name is Rags and. . . ." Joey almost choked as he finished his sentence . . . "and he's such a good dog." The
boy laughed and the mother smiled. "Rags is certainly
a good name. I don't want that dog, Mother. He's too
ugly!" Joey felt the tears burning his eyes. He turned
and ran down the street. Rags was thin and scrawny,
and his fur was dull and unbrushed, but that didn't
matter to Joey. Joey loved the little dog.

Joey slushed through the snow, not knowing or
caring where he was going. Rags snuggled up against
him and helped to keep him warm. Suddenly Joey saw
a Christmas tree in the window of a large brick house.
The Christmas tree was just as pretty as the ones in
the store windows. He walked up the path and peeked
into the window. The lovely green boughs of the Christmas tree were decorated with ornaments of gay colors,
and they spread over beautifully wrapped gifts. Joey
looked at the smiling angel on top. "The people who
live here certainly must be happy," thought Joey. "I'll
bet they'd be good to Rags." He rang the doorbell, and
after a moment's wait the door opened. Joey was silent.
He had hardly been aware of what he was doing and
when a lady appeared at the door, he had absolutely
no idea of what to say or do. "Would you like this dog?
His name is Rags," is what Joey finally blurted out.
He could hear children fighting inside. The lady said,
"What would we want with such a dog?" and shut
the door.

Joey stood before the closed door, speechless. How
could anyone with such a beautiful Christmas tree and

nice house be so grouchy and impolite? Joey slowly
walked down the path. Well, he was glad that they
didn't want Rags. They seemed like such a grumpy
family they probably wouldn't love Rags at all. Rags
began to get restless and Joey decided that he had
better hurry and give him to someone. It got a little
bit harder each time. Resolutely he walked to the door
of the next house. He could smell spicy cookies and he
could hear gay music. "These people must be happy,"
he thought as he pushed the doorbell. This time a teen-
aged girl answered the door. "This is my dog, Rags,"
said Joey. "Would you take him? We can't keep him
anymore." The girl smiled, but her reply was firm.
"We really have no use for a dog." Just then a little
girl streaked through the hall with a boy about Joey's
age in pursuit. He gave the little girl a swat that sent
her rolling on the floor, and screams followed. "My
goodness," thought Joey as the door closed, "these people can't be happy at all. If I treated Connie like that,
we certainly wouldn't have any fun." He was glad that
these people didn't want Rags either.

Joey went to the next house. A man came to the
door, and when he heard what Joey wanted, he laughed.
"Ella," he said to the lady in the next room, "this little
boy wants to give us a dog."

"A what?" asked the lady, and then she began to
laugh, too. The man slammed the door so hard it almost hit Joey in the face. He turned and ran and ran
and ran. He slid twice in the snow, but was up again
each time, still clutching Rags. He finally burst into his
own little house and fell exhausted and sobbing into his
mother's arms. At the sight of Rags, Connie squealed
with delight. The mother was wise enough not to question Joey at that time. She took his wet clothes off and
put his warm pajamas on him. Then she gave him a
bowl of steaming hot porridge. Still sobbing, Joey said,

"Nobody loved Rags, Mother. All the people have pretty Christmas trees and many presents and good food to eat and nice houses to live in, and they all have warm winter coats, but none of them are happy. They could probably give Rags better food, but we love him. Don't make me give him away, Mother, please don't. I can go without a winter coat."

On Christmas morning while Mother read them the Christmas story from the Bible, Connie and Joey sat in their cold little house with Rags between them. As Joey heard the humble story of the birth of Christ, he knew that pretty Christmas trees or presents or expensive food or nice homes didn't make people happy. It was love. And then Joey knew that they were the happiest family in the city: Mother, Joey, Connie, and Rags.

CREATE GOOD FEELINGS AND HAPPINESS

Not only are stories an effective teaching medium, but they can set the stage for better feelings and happiness in families so that the Spirit of the Lord can dwell in the home and so that lessons can be taught.

A lovely young mother told me about her grandmother who had eleven children and managed so well that they grew up in a happy, harmonious home. The young mother wondered what the secret was. She learned that it happened like this in Grandmother's home:

One day the sons who were supposed to be sawing wood were quarreling. The mother was hurrying to prepare a dinner for church officials, but she stopped and went out and sat on a block of wood near where the boys were sawing, and said the magic words: "Let me tell you a story." Soon thereafter the mother and sons were laughing together. Later when the mother went inside, the boys resumed their work without any thought of what they had been quarreling about.

This mother, now a grandmother, took the time to create the happiness and harmony which were in her home. How magic the words can be: "Let me tell you a story. . . ."

CAUSE A BEHAVIORAL CHANGE

It's a tremendously challenging experience to raise a family, and parents are often perplexed by problems and wonder just how to handle them. Stories, either original ones created by the parents or those gleaned from other sources, can frequently meet a need and help solve a family problem. Bad language, telling falsehoods, taking things which don't belong to one, unwillingness to work, sassiness, and untidiness are some of the typical problems which appropriate stories can help correct. Following are sample stories which we have repeated many times in our home to help them become part of our children's lives.

The Story of Three Families

Once upon a time there were three families that lived next door to one another in houses just alike. Not only were their houses alike, but the families themselves were alike—except for one thing. In each family there were a father, a mother, a girl, a boy, and a baby. The fathers all went to work early each morning. The mothers all stayed home during the day to clean, cook, sew, iron, and tend the children. The children went to the same school, and the babies played together. Now, I suppose you're wondering what it was that made these families different.

One family was called the Charles Clutter family,

the second was the Carl Careless family, and the third was the Timothy Tidy family. Now do you know what made these families different from each other?

The Charles Clutter family lived in a pretty house. At least it was pretty when they first moved into it. But whenever the children came home from school, they would just throw their coats, hats, and mittens on the nearest chair—and sometimes these articles even landed on the floor. They put their schoolbooks down wherever they happened to be, and often the baby got into the papers and scattered and tore them. If they went to the kitchen for a snack, they left the milk on the table (where it got sour and had to be thrown away) and the cracker box open on the cupboard. They set the dirty glasses on the drainboard, or sometimes they even carried their snack into their rooms and left the empty glass in there. Whenever they played games, they left them out until pretty soon the parts were lost or ruined. When getting ready for bed at night, they dropped their clothes wherever they happened to be, and pretty soon they didn't have any clean clothes to put on—and those that were clean were wrinkled and needed ironing—and even if some were both clean and pressed, they couldn't find them in all that clutter anyway. The baby's toys were scattered all over and so he seldom played with them because he couldn't find what he wanted. One time Mr. Clutter even broke his ankle because he stepped on some toys on the stairway and fell.

The worst part of the story is that Mr. and Mrs. Clutter were no better than their children. Mr. Clutter always dropped his briefcase anywhere he chose when he came home from work and threw his hat on the living-room couch (where somebody sat on it and ruined it). He laid his tools down all over the house, and pretty soon it was so hard to find them again that

he didn't fix the broken screen or the leaky faucet or
the broken toys.

Mrs. Clutter left her sewing all over and misplaced the dishes and the groceries and the clean
clothes. If a button came off anything, it always got
lost until all the clothes were pinned instead of but-
toned. And sometimes they couldn't even find a pin,
and then they did look awful! She seldom did the housework because it was too much bother to pick up everything so she could vacuum or dust or sweep. She had
a terrible time when shopping because she didn't know
whether they were really out of things at home or
whether she couldn't find them. One time she left some
medicine where it shouldn't be, and the baby ate it.
Then they had to take him to the hospital.

Well, you can imagine what kind of family this
turned out to be. They were always so busy looking
for things that they didn't have time for any fun. And
they were all unhappy and angry all the time and the
children never brought their friends home to their cluttered house. They were embarrassed whenever anyone
came because the house was such a mess. And pretty
soon their house looked like this:

and they looked like this:

The Carl Careless family was just like the Charles Clutter family except that Mrs. Careless really did care about keeping everything orderly. So she spent all day long following the rest of the family around and picking up after them. Of course, she kept telling the rest of the family that they should be more careful, and sometimes she'd even yell at them to try and make them be more orderly. She was always tired and cranky from doing so much work that she never had time to do the things she really wanted to do. The children didn't like to be told the same things over and over again, and so they didn't spend any more time at home than they had to. Even Mr. Careless didn't like coming home after work to a wife that was so tired and cross all the time. So even though their house looked like this:

they looked like this:

The third family, the Timothy Tidy family, was entirely different from the Careless and Clutter families. When the children came home from school, they found it was just as easy to hang up their wraps neatly on hooks in their closets as to throw them on chairs. And they put their books on a special shelf in their rooms where the baby couldn't get into them. Their mother didn't mind if they had a snack because they always cleaned up afterwards. When they wanted to play a game, they knew just where to find it, and they enjoyed the same games for many years because the pieces were never lost or broken. It only took them a few minutes to get ready for school in the mornings because their clothes were always clean and pressed and hanging in their closets. Mr. Tidy never left his briefcase and hat where they could be ruined or misplaced, and he kept his tools in a special place so he could always find them. Mrs. Tidy kept the house shining clean and never left anything out where the baby could get into it. She only had to spend a few hours a day doing the housework, and then she could spend the rest of her time doing special things for her family. Best of all, she was always cheerful and happy, and her children and husband loved to be at home with her. The children were always proud to bring their friends home, and when the doorbell rang, they could enjoy having company come without being embarrassed. And the funny part is that it took the Tidy family much less time to be Tidy than it took the Clutter and Careless families to be cluttered and careless. And the Tidy family's house always looked like this:

And they looked like this:

Which family should we be like?

Project Tidiness: Give each family member 25 beans in a little bag or jar. During the week, whenever someone of the family finds an object out of place, he picks it up and "sells" it back to the person it belongs to for one bean. At the end of the week, the one having the most beans gets a special treat or reward. Since tidiness is more habit than anything else, this game could be continued until the tidiness habit is solidly formed among all family members.

HONESTY

Suggested approach: retold story (use vocabulary on
   age level of child)

The Necklace of Truth

There was once a little girl by the name of Coralie, who took pleasure in telling falsehoods. Some children think very little of not speaking the truth; and a small falsehood, or a great one in case of necessity, that saves them from a duty or a punishment, seems to them the most allowable thing in the world. Now Coralie was one of this sort. The truth was a thing of which she had no idea; and any excuse was good to her, provided that it was believed. For a long time, her parents were deceived by her stories; but they saw at last that she was telling them what was not true, and from that moment they had not the least confidence in anything that she said. It is a terrible thing for parents not to be able to believe their children's words.

After vainly trying every means to reform her, Coralie's parents resolved to take her to the enchanter Merlin, who was celebrated at that time over all the globe, and who was the greatest friend of truth that ever lived. For this reason, little children that were in the habit of telling falsehoods, were brought to him from all directions, in order that he might cure them.

The enchanter Merlin lived in a glass palace, the walls of which were transparent; and never in his whole life had the idea crossed his mind of disguising one of his actions, or causing others to believe what was not true. He knew liars a league off; and when Coralie approached the palace, he knew what was the matter.

Coralie's mother, with a beating heart, undertook to

explain why she had come, but she was so ashamed that she could hardly talk. Merlin stopped her short.

"I know what is the matter, my good lady," said he. "I felt your daughter's approach long ago. She is one of the greatest liars in the world, and she has made me very uncomfortable."

The parents knew that fame had not deceived them in praising the skill of the enchanter; and Coralie, covered with confusion, knew not where to hide her head. She took refuge under the apron of her mother, who sheltered her as well as she could, while her father stood before her to protect her at all risks. They were very anxious that their child should be cured, but they wished her cured gently and without hurting her.

"Don't be afraid," said Merlin, seeing their terror. "I do not employ violence in curing these diseases. I am only going to make Coralie a beautiful present, which I think will not displease her."

He opened a drawer, and took from it a magnificent amethyst necklace, beautifully set, with a diamond clasp of dazzling lustre. He put it on Coralie's neck, and dismissing the parents with a friendly gesture, "Go, good people," said he, "and have no more anxiety. Your daughter carries with her a sure guardian of the truth."

Coralie, flushed with pleasure, was hastily retreating, delighted at having escaped so easily, when Merlin called her back.

"In a year," said he, looking at her sternly, "I shall come for my necklace. Till that time I forbid you to take it off for a single instant; if you dare to do so, woe be unto you!"

"Oh, I ask nothing better than always to wear it—it is so beautiful."

In order that you may know, I will tell you that this necklace was none other than the famous Necklace of Truth, so much talked of in ancient books, which unveiled every species of falsehood.

The day after Coralie returned home she was sent to school. As she had long been absent, all the little girls crowded around her, as always happens in such cases. There was a general cry of admiration at the sight of the necklace.

"Where did it come from?" and "Where did you get it?" was asked on all sides.

In those days, for any one to say that he .had been to
the enchanter Merlin was to tell the whole story. Coralie
took good care not to betray herself in this way.

"I was sick for a long time," said she, boldly; "and on
my recovery, my parents gave me this beautiful necklace."

A loud cry rose from all at once. The diamonds of the
clasp, which had shot forth so brilliant a light, had suddenly
become dim, and were turned to coarse glass.

"Well, yes I have been sick! What are you making such
a fuss about?"

At this second falsehood, the amethysts in turn changed
to ugly yellow stones. A new cry arose. Coralie, seeing all
eyes fixed on her necklace, looked that way herself, and was
struck with terror.

"I have been to the enchanter Merlin," she said, humbly,
understanding from what direction the blow came, and not
daring to persist in her falsehood.

Scarcely had she confessed the truth when the necklace
recovered all its beauty; but the loud bursts of laughter that
sounded around her, mortified her to such a degree, that
she felt the need of saying something to retrieve her
reputation.

"You do very wrong to laugh," said she, "for he treated
us with the greatest possible respect. He sent his carriage
to meet us at the next town, and you have no idea what a
splendid carriage it was—six white horses, pink satin cushions
with gold tassels, to say nothing of the coachman with his
hair powdered, and the three tall footmen behind! When we
reached his palace, which is of jasper, he came to meet us at
the vestibule, and led us to the dining-room, where stood a
table covered with things that I will not name to you, because
you never even heard speak of them. There was, in the first
place—"

The laughter, which had been suppressed with great
difficulty ever since she commenced this fine story, became
at that moment so boisterous that she stopped in amazement;
and casting her eyes once more on the unlucky necklace, she
shuddered anew. At each detail that she invented, the necklace had become longer and longer, until it already dragged on
the ground.

"You are stretching the truth," cried the little girls.

"Well, I confess it; we went on foot, and only stayed five minutes."

The necklace instantly shrank to its proper size.

"And the necklace—the necklace—where did it come from?"

"He gave it to me without saying a word; probably—"

She had not time to finish. The fatal necklace grew shorter and shorter till it choked her terribly, and she gasped for want of breath.

"You are keeping back part of the truth," cried her school-fellows.

She hastened to alter the broken words while she could still speak.

"He said—that I was—one of the greatest—liars—in the world."

Instantly freed from the pressure that was strangling her, she continued to cry with pain and mortification.

"That was why he gave me the necklace. He said that it was a guardian of truth, and I have been a great fool to be proud of it. Now I am in a fine position!"

Her little companions felt sorry for her; for they were good girls, and they thought how they should feel in her place. You can imagine, indeed, that it was somewhat embarrassing for a girl to know that she could never more hide the truth.

"You are very good," said one of them. "If I were in your place, I should soon send back the necklace; handsome as it is, it is a great deal too troublesome. What hinders you from taking it off?"

Poor Coralie was silent; but the stones began to dance up and down, and to make a terrible clatter.

"There is something that you have not told us," said the little girls, their merriment restored by this extraordinary dance.

"I like to wear it."

The diamonds and amethysts danced and clattered worse than ever.

"There is a reason which you are hiding from us."

"Well, since I can conceal nothing from you, he forbade me to take it off, under penalty of some great calamity."

You can imagine that with a companion of this kind, which turned dull whenever the wearer did not tell the truth, which grew longer whenever she added to it, which shrank whenever she subtracted from it, and which danced and clattered whenever she was silent,—a companion, moreover, of which she could not rid herself,—it was impossible even for the most hardened liar not to keep closely to the truth. When Coralie once was fully convinced that falsehood was useless, and that it would be instantly discovered, it was not difficult for her to abandon it. The consequence was, that when she became accustomed always to tell the truth, she found herself so happy in it—she felt her conscience so light and her mind so calm—that she began to hate falsehood for its own sake, and the necklace had nothing more to do. Long before the year passed, therefore, Merlin came for his necklace, which he needed for another child that was given to lying, and which, thanks to his art, he knew was of no more use to Coralie.

No one can tell me what has become of this wonderful Necklace of Truth; but it is thought that Merlin's heirs hid it after his death, for fear of the ravages that it might cause on earth. You can imagine what a calamity it would be to many people—I do not speak only of children—if they were forced to wear it. Some travelers who have returned from Central Africa declare that they have seen it on the neck of a king, who knew not how to lie; but they have never been able to prove their words. Search is still being made for it, however; and if I were a little child in the habit of telling falsehoods, I should not feel quite sure that it might not some day be found again.

(From Mace's *Fairy Book,* by Jean Mace, translated by Mary L. Booth. Reprinted by permission of Harper & Row, Publishers, Inc.)

DURFEY AND DISHONESTY

Note to parents: All children love puppet shows. They enjoy watching them, they adore inventing their own characters and plot, and they delight in putting on the final production. It is wise to take advantage of the children's love of puppets and let the puppets become their teachers. You can be sure the children will listen to what the puppets tell them!

The puppets can be homemade with heads made from styrofoam, potatoes, papier mache, clay, or anything else appropriate. Other kinds of puppets can be made from scraps of material sewn in the shape of a head, two arms, and a body, with the face painted right on the material. The stores carry many adorable puppets if you prefer to buy them.

The puppet stage can be very simple to very elaborate. To make a simple stage, cut a window in one side of a cardboard box. To make it more elaborate, decorate the box with paint, paper or contact paper; sew curtains and make stage props. It is up to you to decide how much you want to do.

Make the characters as delightful as possible through exaggerated facial expressions and exciting costumes. Disguised voices add to the effectiveness of the show. After the children have practised the show, let them present it at the next family night. They may change the script in any way they choose so long as the message remains the same.

The puppet show we have developed on the following pages is concerned with the subject of honesty. It deals with taking only that which belongs to one.

Suggested approach: puppet show presentation

Materials needed: two puppets, puppet stage, wallet, and one dollar bill.

Oscar: Oh, hello there, children! My name is Oscar

Honest. I'm just waiting here for my friend Durfey Dishonest. We always walk to school together. I'm especially excited to see him today because last night I helped Mr. Frost clean out his garage. He paid me a dollar for it so now I have enough money to buy the truck in the drugstore. Durfey and I both want trucks, and we decided to buy them as soon as we both earned the money. Oh, here comes Durfey now. Excuse me please, will you? I want to tell him about this on my way to school.

Durfey: Hi there, Oscar old pal. What's new?

Oscar: How come you're so late, Durfey? I've been waiting for you.

Durfey: Aw, gee. My mom made me make my bed before coming to school, and she says I have to hurry right home afterwards to practise my piano lesson. Gee whiz. I sure wish I didn't have to bother with all that stuff.

Oscar: Oh, well. Come on and let's hurry now. Besides, I've got some good news to tell you. I worked for Mr. Frost last night and earned a dollar. Have you got your money yet?

Durfey: Gosh, no. I asked Mom if she'd lend me the money but she wouldn't. She said I'd have to find a job around the neighborhood and earn it. I sure don't feel like doing that.

Oscar: You want a truck, don't you?

Durfey: Sure I do. We could have lots of fun if we both got trucks. We could build a highway system in that vacant lot next to our place and make tunnels and bridges and everything. It sure would be neat.

Oscar: Hey! What's that over there by the fence?

	It looks like a wallet. I wonder who lost it?
Durfey:	(picking it up) It sure is beat-up. I wonder if there's anything in it. Come on, let's see.
Oscar:	There's the name. It says Johnny Nichols. He's in your room at school, isn't he?
Durfey:	Sure is. Let's see what else is in it. Some notes, a key chain, some pictures. Hey! Look! Here's a dollar bill all folded up in the corner. Boy! That sure is terrific. Now we can both get our trucks right after school today.
Oscar:	But Durfey. That isn't your money. You wouldn't really keep it, would you? Especially when you know whom it belongs to.
Durfey:	Haven't you ever heard of "finders keepers." I'll put the wallet right back where we found it and just keep the money. It's not like I was taking the whole thing—just the dollar. Nobody will know the difference.
Oscar:	You'll know, Durfey. That's being dishonest.
Durfey:	Gee whiz, Oscar. It's only a dollar. The police sure aren't going to worry about that.
Oscar:	Oh, oh. There's the school bell. We'd better run or we'll be late. You'd better put the money back and return the wallet to Johnny.
Durfey:	No, sir. I'll leave the wallet right here. Come on, let's hurry. I'll see you at lunchtime and we'll make plans for buying the trucks.

(Scene two—lunchtime)

Oscar:	Hi, Durfey! Let's hurry and eat so we can play baseball during the lunch hour.
Durfey:	(dejected) All right.

Oscar: What are you so glum about? I thought you wanted to make plans for our trucks.

Durfey: Yeah. But this morning sure has been lousy. Johnny kept looking at me just like he was accusing me of something. And every time the teacher stopped by my desk I was sure she was looking right straight into my pocket to see if I had that dollar bill in there.

Oscar: You're just imagining it, Durfey. It's just your guilty conscience. I told you you'd be sorry. Why don't you go get the wallet after we're through with lunch. You could still return it.

Durfey: It's too late now. Miss Williams excused Johnny from class this morning long enough to go look for his wallet. He found it all right, just where we'd left it.

Oscar: Except, of course, it didn't have the dollar in it.

Durfey: (defiantly) Well, I'm still not sorry I took it. We'll have lots of fun with our trucks. Come on, let's eat.

(Scene three—after school)

Durfey: Let's hurry and get our trucks, Oscar.

Oscar: I thought you had to go straight home.

Durfey: I do, but Mom will never know if we hurry. Come on, let's go.

Oscar: Durfey, are you sure you want to spend that dollar?

Durfey: Don't you want me to have a truck, too?

Oscar: Sure, but. . . .

Durfey: All right then, let's go buy them. Besides, I got to figuring. The trucks are only 69c each. We'll have enough left over for a chocolate malt.

Durfey: Hey! That's right. That's a neat idea. Let's go then.

(Scene four—next morning on the way to school)

Oscar: Hi, Durfey. Wow, did I have fun last night with my truck. I built a long ramp down the stairs and let it whiz all the way to the bottom. I even got my little brother to bring it back up to me each time so I didn't have to go down after it. What did you do with yours?

Durfey: Gee whiz, Oscar. You know I couldn't play with mine at home. My folks would want to know where I got it from. Then what would I say?

Oscar: Well, if you can't play with it at home, it's not much fun having it. It sure was stupid of you to take that dollar anyway.

Durfey: Well, it's too late now to do anything. At least I don't have to practise my piano tonight. I got it done this morning so we could start building our highways tonight.

Oscar: Good, maybe we'll have time at lunch to draw a map so we can start building right after school.

Durfey: Aw gee, that reminds me. Miss Williams is making me stay in at lunchtime today to help her. She says it's because I'm such a good worker, but I think she's just trying to punish me.

Oscar: What is she punishing you for, Durfey?

Durfey: She knows I took that dollar. She's just trying to get even with me.

Oscar: That's just your imagination again, Durfey.
          Or I should say guilty conscience. I'm glad
          I earned my truck so I can enjoy it.
Durfey: Well, never mind. I'll see you right after
          school.

(Scene five—after school)

Oscar: Come on, Durfey. Let's hurry and change
          our clothes so we can play.
Durfey: Aw, you go on Oscar. I don't think I'm going
          to play tonight. Who wants to build a stupid
          highway, anyway—or play with silly trucks
          for that matter.
Oscar: What do you mean by that? It was your
          idea in the first place. I think it's just your
          guilty conscience again.
Durfey: Oscar, I know you don't believe it, but every-
          one knows I took that dollar. Today when
          Miss Williams was collecting fees for our
          field trip next week Johnny told her all about
          losing his money for it. He looked right at
          me the whole time. Anyway, Johnny's
          father is in the hospital right now and he
          says his folks can't give him any more money
          for the field trip so he's going to stay home.
Oscar: He could earn some before then, couldn't he?
Durfey: That's what Miss Williams asked him. But
          he said he already works after school and
          on Saturdays at the grocery store stocking
          shelves. He said all that money has to go
          to his parents to help out right now, and he
          just wouldn't feel right keeping out a dollar.
          I sure wish I hadn't taken that dollar.
Oscar: I told you so, Durfey.
Durfey: And then on top of that Miss Williams gave

us our new spelling list today. The very first
word was wallet. And the next to last one
was dollar. She's just trying to make me
squirm.

Oscar: It's just your guilty conscience, Durfey. It's
plain to see you're not going to be happy
until you give that dollar back to Johnny.

Durfey: You know I can't do that.

Oscar: Why can't you, Durfey?

Durfey: Then he'd know for sure I stole it. Besides,
I've already spent it.

Oscar: I was going to help Mr. Frost clean his base-
ment tonight. I'll let you do it if you'll promise to give the money to Johnny.

Durfey: Gee . . . I don't know, Oscar. Maybe Johnny
would report me or something.

Oscar: Even if he did you would feel better than
you do now. And if you're really sincerely
sorry, I bet Johnny won't tell a person.
That's the only way you'll be happy. It's
a sure cinch that truck isn't any good to you
the way it is.

Durfey: Well . . . . Would you come with me?

Oscar: If you want me to. I'd kind of like to see
Johnny's face when you return it to him. I
bet he'll be the happiest guy around.

Durfey: What time am I supposed to be at Mr. Frost's
to help him?
Six o'clock. Don't be late and be sure to do a
good job or Mr. Frost will be mad at me for
sending you instead.

Durfey: I will, Oscar. I promise. And . . . well
. . . . . thanks a lot, Oscar. I'll see you tomorrow at ten. We can go find Johnny then. Be
sure to meet me.

Oscar: I will Durfey. See you at ten.

          (Scene six)

Oscar: Oh, hello again, children? I just came back
          from Johnny's place with Durfey. It sure
          was hard for Durfey to admit he'd taken
          that money, but he did it and I was real
          happy about it. Do you remember when I
          said I would like to see Johnny's face? Well,
          Johnny looked pretty happy all right. But
          Durfey looked even happier. And I know
          something else. Durfey really learned his
          lesson this time. He'll never again take
          something that doesn't belong to him. Be-
          sides being dishonest, it just isn't worth all
          the unhappiness and trouble.

MISS MINNIE-MIND-YOUR-MANNERS

Suggested approach: The poem should be used as an
          introduction to a discussion on manners, and as a
          means of introducing Miss Minnie-Mind-Your-

Manners. After the children have heard the poem,
it would be good to make a list of the rules suggested and then add to it as you would like to.
Let the children review all the rules listed and
perhaps ask them to memorize the fifth verse,
("Good manners are simply doing, in the very
nicest way, The best and kindest thing we know,
All day long, each single day.")

Materials needed: Miss Minnie-Mind-Your-Manners
(See kit)

With your encouragement, a very good friendship
will grow between Miss Minnie-Mind-Your-Manners
and your children! Use Miss Minnie extensively for a
week and from then on only occasionally as the children need reminding.

MANNERS

We see so many people
In the things we do each day,
We hope these people like us
And all we do and say.

We want to let them know
We'd like them for a friend,
And that we'll do whate'er we can
To be a friend to them.

So what, do you think, is the very first thing
We must be sure to do,
If we want people to say to us
"My goodness, I surely like you."

. . . HAVE GOOD MANNERS

So now we know what the secret is
That will always help us go far
In making friends and keeping them.
Now—what do you think good manners are?

Good manners are simply doing
In the very nicest way
The best and kindest thing we know
All day long, each single day.

Good manners are using the magic words
As often as we should,
Whenever someone is nice to us
Or does anything that's good.

And what would you guess are these magic words
That we must always remember
To use often each day of the year
From January to December?

. . . PLEASE AND THANK YOU

But having good manners is much more than this.
There are many rules we must follow.
So let's decide now to learn what they are
And start practising them for tomorrow.

When guests arrive it's the polite thing to do
To give them prompt attention
Shake hands, smile, and say, "We're glad you are here."
And turn off that TV invention!

Another good rule that's important for you
As a child to immediately learn,
Is never interrupt what others are saying
And speak only when it's your turn.

Telephone manners are fun to know
Be sure to answer politely.
Speak loudly enough for the caller to hear
And make sure you do everything rightly.

Has a new child moved into your neighborhood?
If so, welcome him with a smile
Invite him to join in your games and your fun
You'll find this effort worthwhile.

Classes in school or church can be fun
But what must we first understand?

Listen carefully as the teacher talks
And if you talk, first raise your hand.

While playing with friends at home or at school
We must always, yes always, be fair,
We'll have twice as much fun in whatever we do
If we'll only remember to SHARE.

Chewing gum is a pleasure and candy's a treat,
But not nice to do around others,
Unless you have plenty to share with each one
Including your sisters and brothers!

When visiting friends and away from home
Be sure to act ever so nicely.
Don't run, jump or shout or touch things that you shouldn't
And when leaving say "thank you" politely.

But manners are not just for friends and for guests
Don't ever think that—goodness me!
Manners are especially important at home
With your very own family!

So tonight we're meeting a brand new friend
Who will help us remember to be
The best-mannered children you ever will know
In the best-mannered family.

Meet MISS MINNIE-MIND-YOUR-MANNERS

Miss Minnie has come to visit this week
With us she'll spend several days,
When we forget the rules we have learned
She'll show us her frowning face.

But when we're polite and kind and good
And show her our very best style,
Of being well-mannered all the day through
Then watch Miss Minnie *smile!*

MISS MINNIE MIND-YOUR-MANNERS

To make Miss Minnie-Mind-Your-Manners, cut one side out of a square cardboard box, and tape remaining three sides together, forming a three-sided box. Cover with butcher paper and draw three faces as illustrated above, one on each side of the box.

Let Miss Minnie-Mind-Your-Manners eat with your family for a week, as well as participate in other activities. While she is watching you, she shows her second face. When your manners are poor, she turns her first face to you. When your manners are very good, you see face number three.

See how often you can make Miss Minnie-Mind-Your-Manners smile this week! And be sure to put her to bed each each night showing the face which best describes your day! We hope she smiles in her sleep every night! And do you know what? When Miss Minnie-Mind-Your Manners is smiling, you'll be smiling too because having good manners makes you happy!

SHARING

A Brother Like That

Suggested approach: retold story and family activities

A friend of mine named Paul received a new automobile from his brother as a pre-Christmas present. On Christmas Eve, when Paul came out of his office, a street urchin was walking around the shiny new car, admiring it. "Is this your new car, mister?" he asked.

Paul nodded. "My brother gave it to me for Christmas."

The boy looked astounded. "You mean your brother gave it to you, and it didn't cost you nothing? Gosh, I wish. . . ."

He hesitated, and Paul knew what he was going to wish. He was going to wish he had a brother like that. But what the lad said jarred Paul all the way down to his heels. "I wish," the boy went on, "that I could *be* a brother like that."

Paul looked at the boy in astonishment, then impulsively he added, "Would you like to ride in my automobile?"

"Oh, yes, I'd love that!"

After a short ride the urchin turned, and with his eyes aglow said, "Mister, would you mind driving in front of my house?"

Paul smiled a little. He thought he knew what the lad wanted. He wanted to show his neighbors that he could ride home in a big automobile. But Paul was wrong again.

"Will you stop right where those two steps are?" the boy asked.

He ran up the steps. Then in a little while Paul heard him coming back, but he was not coming fast. He was carrying his little polio-crippled brother. He sat him down on the bottom step, then sort of squeezed up against him, and pointed to the car.

"There she is, Buddy, just like I told you upstairs. His brother give it to him for Christmas, and it didn't cost him a cent, and someday I'm gonna give you one just like it; then you can see for yourself all the pretty things in the Christmas windows that I've been trying to tell you about."

Paul got out and lifted the little lad to the front seat of his car. The shining eyed older brother climbed in beside him and the three of them began a memorable holiday ride.

That Christmas Eve Paul learned what Jesus meant when he said:

"It is more blessed to give. . . ."

—C. Roy Angell
from *Baskets of Silver*
(Boardman Press)

To help every child want to be "a brother like that" should be one of the foremost values parents strive to cultivate in their children. Sermons and words alone cannot help a child feel the joy of service; they must experience it for themselves. Parents can help greatly by providing some of these experiences; for instance, one evening after our children had baked and decorated several dozen Valentine cookies and had delivered them to neighbor children, our four-year-old daughter prayed at bedtime: "I thank thee for the loveliest day I've ever had."

Family hours can afford an ideal time to encourage children in planning and carrying out ways to share or participate in service projects. Here are some suggested activities:

Children can help bake and decorate goodies for friends, neighbors, and cousins at holiday time. (Even though most of the work falls on Mother, the children catch the spirit of it!) For instance, heart-shaped cookies can be delivered as Valentines; bunnies made from snowballs (round balls of cake frosted in white or pink and sprinkled with coconut purchased at the cupcake and cookie counter of the grocery store) with colored toothpick whiskers, cinnamon candy eyes and nose, and pink paper ears are delightful for friends at Easter time; caramel apples or cupcakes decorated in orange and brown are fun for Halloween; cookies, gingerbread men, pastries, baskets of fruit are just some of the lovely things to share at Christmas. Projects along this line help shift the thoughts of children from "what am I going to get" to "what can I give."

Gift giving can be more meaningful and satisfying to a child if he can make himself or purchase with money he has earned, things for others.

Children are able to gain through the efforts of making their own greeting cards, birthday cards, and Valentines. We have enjoyed finger painting, splatter painting, and block painting, as means to decorate cards.

The way could be provided for children to participate in a "Sub for Santa" drive and become aware that there are those who are less fortunate and who need help. Perhaps a family could provide an entire Christmas for some needy family, even if it means limiting their own Christmas presents. We don't share only when we have an excess of something; the true spirit of sharing lies in giving something when it is not so easy—when it hurts a little. It is good for children sometimes truly to feel a material loss through sharing with others. In this way they can learn that to sacrifice is to give up something good for something better.

Occasionally a child could use part of his allowance or money he has earned to help someone else.

When little friends become ill and are bedridden for a time, wouldn't it be a delightful experience to prepare a box of surprises and suggestions for sick-bed activities for them!

One family raises a garden for the purpose of sharing vegetables and flowers with others.

A blind girl lived in our neighborhood as I grew up. We teenage girls used to take turns reading her lessons to her after school. This was one of the most humbling and satisfying experiences of my life.

A group of girls were planning a week at summer camp. One blind girl wasn't able to go until a thoughtful friend in the group offered to be her eyes for a week.

Young girls can extend voluntary baby-sitting services to mothers who are in need of special help or who are engaged in church or community service.

Boys can help widows or other needy neighbors by doing yard work, shoveling snow, carrying out garbage, or running errands.

And, most important of all, a child must learn to

give of himself—a smile; a kind word; an edifying thought; a understanding heart; a listening ear; a word of praise; an expression of gratitude; a bit of cheer or sincere, loyal friendship and true love.

TRUSTWORTHINESS

Suggested approach: retold story

Materials needed: five envelopes with slips of paper inside

FIVE ENVELOPES AND A JOB

For the third time that morning Jay Lawford reached for his spelling book and took from it a small piece of paper he had clipped from the "Help Wanted" column of the morning paper.   And for the third time he read: "Boy between ten and twelve wanted for work after school and on Saturday. Good wages if trustworthy and dependable.   Apply today at 4:15 p.m., Mason & Company, Jewelers, 34 Madison Avenue." If he could only get that job he could buy a bicycle and then later a radio set!

When school was out he raced home and carefully got himself cleaned up, then he walked down to Mason and Company's store.

He opened their door at just twelve minutes after four and saw seven other boys standing near the office door.   Just as one of the beautiful chime clocks in the store announced that it was 4:15 this door was opened from the inside by a small oldish gentleman who said in a voice that sounded as pleasant as his chime clock, "Come in, boys; I am Mr. Mason."

The boys went in.   Some sat down in chairs at once; some including Jay, stood until Mr. Mason said, "Be seated, boys."

For the next few minutes the pleasant old jeweler talked about play and studies and asked each boy a question or two

about which game he liked best or what study he was most
interested in.

Someone knocked at the office door and as Mr. Mason
opened it, Jay saw four more boys standing outside. "No,
boys, no. I am sorry, but 4:15 does not mean 4:30," said
Mr. Mason, as he shut the door again.

After a few more minutes of talking and asking questions, Mr. Mason stood up and touching one boy, said: "This
boy," then another, "and this boy," and then putting his hand
on Jay's shoulder, "and this boy, please stay. Thanks to all
of you for coming and good afternoon." He opened the door
and let the other boys go out.

The jeweler asked the three remaining boys to write
their names on a paper, and then he said, "Now, then, Donald,
Herman, and Jay, tomorrow being Saturday and no school,
I want you here promptly at nine. You will each be busy
all day, though not at real work, and will be paid for a day's
work. I will write on paper what you are to do; the one who
does what he is told will get the job, and whoever gets the
job will be well paid. That is all; see you tomorrow." And
the boys were out in the street wondering what it was all
about.

The next morning at 9:00 o'clock the three boys were in
the same private office and the same Mr. Mason was saying,
"Of course a jeweler has to be very careful in selecting people
to work for him, and we all have different ways of finding
the person we want. I am giving each of you boys a large
envelope; in it are five small envelopes numbered from 1 to
5. When you go out you will open the large envelope and take
out No. 1; tear it open and read what you are to do. Here
is money for each of you. It will cover your expenses and
pay you for the day's time. You may happen to meet each
other during the day, but do not talk if you do. Read the
instructions and do what you are told. That is all."

The three boys, standing apart from each other on the
sidewalk, each opened his large envelope and then tore open
envelope No. 1. In each was a slip of paper with writing on
it. (To the storyteller: you, yourself, may wish to have the
envelopes and notes to use as you tell the story.)

The paper in Jay's envelope No. 1 read: "Walk to the

corner of Adams and Market Street and wait there until someone tells you to go—then open envelope No. 2."

"This is a simple little thing to do," thought Jay. And though the place was only a few blocks away he lost no time in getting there.

When he reached the corner he waited and waited, and then he began wondering if this were the right place because no one spoke to him and the only person he could see was a policeman nearby. Jay waited a whole half hour and was almost on the point of returning to ask Mr. Mason if he had made a mistake, but he decided to wait a little longer.

Just at eleven o'clock the policeman touched Jay on the shoulder and said to him, "You can go now." So the policeman was one of Mr. Mason's friends and in the game, too?

"What will be the next queer order," he wondered as he quickly tore open envelope No. 2. The note inside said, "Go as quickly as possible to Grant Park and get a leaf from a maple tree there. Then open envelope No. 3."

Jay knew that Grant Park was at least two miles away and that the quickest way to get there was by bus. He walked to the corner where the park busses passed and got on one after only a short wait.

While riding on the bus, he had time to think about the queer test. His thoughts were cut short, however, when he noticed a whole row of maple trees. Why, here were dozens of maple trees! He needn't go all the way to the park and waste so much time, so much time that he might even lose the job—and the bike and the radio. He was about to leave the bus when he remembered what Mr. Mason said about following instructions; and the note plainly told him to go to Grant Park to get the maple leaf. So he could do nothing but sit down and wait.

In the park, Jay dashed to the first maple tree he saw, picked a leaf and put it into the big envelope. He then tore open envelope No. 3 and read: "Stay in the park one hour, then walk to the Grill Restaurant on Washington Street and order a good meal. When the waiter brings it to you, open envelope No. 4."

"Another big wait," said Jay to himself. "I suppose, though, that when Mr. Mason tells anyone to do a certain thing in a certain way he means it, so here goes." And Jay strolled around the green park.

When the hour was up he started off for the business section of the town again, thinking of the good meal he was going to have.

"Say, buddy, hop in and I'll take you along," called out the driver of a bright-colored open car.

"Sure, I'll be glad to . . ." but suddenly Jay remembered the instructions said *"Walk* to the Grill Restaurant," so he stammered, "I-I suppose—I'd like to all right, but I've really got to walk."

"Oh, that's all right," said the driver as he gave Jay a knowing wink. "Why, could it be that this driver was in on the secret, too," wondered Jay as the man smiled, waved his hand, and drove away.

It was long after one o'clock when Jay sat down at a table in the restaurant, tired and very hungry. He had plenty of money to spend on a good meal, and the written directions had said, "a real good meal." So Jay decided to follow the order completely. From the menu card he selected hot corn bread, roast ham with sweet potatoes, apple pie and ice cream. Jay decided this Mr. Mason was really a prince of a good fellow even though he might be a trifle fussy in some ways!

As the waiter placed the dishes before him, Jay thought he had never seen anything look so good as did that yellow corn bread with the golden butter trickling down its side. He was just ready to take a bite when he suddenly remembered that his note said he was to open envelope No. 4 when the waiter brought him his dinner. He took a longing look at the tempting food and then tore open the next envelope and read, "Get up at once, pay the waiter, and go without delay to room 515, Story Building."

Jay took another look at the food, then quickly decided that he was going to do his very best to get that job no matter what he had to go through or give up, so he arose from his chair and asked the waiter for his check.

"Say, bub, what's the meaning of this funny business? You're the third boy today that's ordered a big meal and then pulled out an envelope to read something. One boy was a fat kid; he said he wouldn't leave a good dinner like that for the best job in the world," said the surprised waiter.

Not even stopping to reply to the waiter, Jay paid for

the dinner and, feeling hungrier than ever walked to the Story Building, took the elevator to the fifth floor and then went into room 515. A man sitting at a big desk looked up, smiled at Jay as if he were expecting him and inquired, "Are you one of the boys from Mason's?"

After Jay had answered, the man continued: "Mr. Mason requested me to give each boy that came this envelope No. 5, and to take from you your last envelope numbered 5. Can you guess the reason why?" (To the storyteller: Let the children give reasons.)

Well, Jay thought for a while but was forced to say no, he didn't know.

The man continued, "Some boys, some smart boys, might get the idea that they could save time by opening all of the envelopes at the same time, and then follow only the last instruction. To prevent that, Mr. Mason has given a very different order in the envelope which I am now giving you. Here it is, open it, and do what is told. And, by the way, did you know that most of the people now working for Mr. Mason first went through some hard test to prove their honesty and dependability—their willingness to do what they should do, even under difficult conditions?"

Jay gave the man his envelope No. 5 and tore open the new one. It said, "Walk to the corner of Pine and Adams Street where someone will meet you very soon."

Hoping that after all he might be the fortunate one to get the job, Jay hurried to the corner. When he arrived there he could not see anyone he knew. Was this to be another exasperating delay?

"Good afternoon," said a cheery voice which could belong to no one else than the mysterious Mr. Mason, the jeweler.

"I'll come to the point at once," he continued, laying his hand on Jay's shoulder, "the job is yours! Yours because Herman wouldn't give up that good dinner, and because Donald thought he was so smart he could skip envelope No. 4. As a result he didn't change his last envelope as he should have done—he didn't want to let anyone beat him so he opened envelopes No. 4 and No. 5 together and came back to my store. From that I knew he hadn't followed orders and wouldn't be able to endure the things this job required."

Jay's face was beaming with delight; he was so happy he even forgot how hungry he was. The job was his! And so would be the bicycle and the radio!

"Now, Jay, here are some more instructions," said the pleasant little man, "go right back to the Grill Restaurant— I've told them you are coming—and eat all you want and then come and start working for Mason & Co., Jewelers, of 34 Madison Avenue."

(By Wendell B. Hammond, adapted from *The Chidren's Friend*. Used by permission of the author.)

INSPIRE FAITH

Stories—including experiences and examples— can inspire faith, help children develop an understanding of the gospel, and build testimonies in their hearts.

The Balloon Ride

One day, many, many years ago, an old-fashioned country fair was held. Families for miles around visited the fair. The balloon ride was the big attraction.

Jenny and her family were at the fair, and Jenny was excitedly sitting in the basket of the balloon, awaiting her family and other passengers. Suddenly a gust of wind blew the balloon's rope out of the attendant's hands. Up, up, up it went. The people, river, houses, trees and animals grew smaller and smaller and smaller as Jenny watched from the side of the basket.

Jenny was terribly frightened! In fact she was frantic! What should she do? How high would the balloon go? What was going to happen to her?

Then she knew what to do. Jenny prayed about it. She asked her Heavenly Father what she should do. Soon she noticed a rope and felt impressed to pull it.

As she did so, some of the gas in the balloon was released and the balloon descended just a little. She pulled the rope again, and the balloon went down a little more. She pulled it again and again, each time letting a little more of the gas escape. She felt impressed to pull only a little bit at a time so that the balloon wouldn't go down too fast. As she went lower and lower, she looked over the edge of the basket and saw the people, river, houses, trees, and animals growing larger and larger again. She was almost to the ground! How thrilled and thankful she was.

She landed safely in a meadow not far from the country fair grounds. How happy everyone was to see her. How happy she was to see them! As she hugged her mother, she learned that her parents, too, had prayed. They were grateful to Heavenly Father who had heard and answered their prayers.

MISSIONARY WORK

A Story of Three Boys

Suggested approach: retold stories with personal application

James was born into a Latter-day Saint home, and his parents were active in the Church. Some of his ancestors were among prominent people in the Church. During his high school years, James attended meetings only fairly regularly. He became very interested in a girl named Anne. She wasn't very active, either.

One day a former neighbor of the family met this young couple on the street. She said, "James, you will soon be going on a mission, won't you?"

Anne spoke up and said, "We have decided that James isn't going on a mission. We think it would make such a hole in our lives."

James did not go on a mission. He and Anne married very young. Their life together has been unhappy, and their marriage is unsuccessful.

"It would make such a hole in our lives. . . ."

* * *

Reed was also born into a Latter-day Saint home. At the time of his birth, during World War II, the doctor said, "You have a little general."

His parents thought, "No, we have a little missionary."

Among the gifts given to this baby was a silver dollar to start his missionary fund. This was the beginning of a growing fund for him. Reed saved part of his allowance and the money he earned for his mission. He had a special bank for this purpose.

Reed attended church faithfully and honored the priesthood which had been given him. He went to seminary and learned all he could about the gospel. He studied a foreign language in school. During the six months he was in the armed service, he devoted much of his spare time to studying the scriptures and reading about the gospel.

He enjoyed missionary farewells and homecomings, always with his mission in mind.

His mission was part of his dreams and part of all his planning. It was part of his conversation. It was natural and easy for him to be prepared in every way when his call came.

Reed found that after one gains a testimony, it becomes a compelling desire to share that testimony

with others. So it was with Andrew and Simon, the
ancient apostles who were taught by Jesus Christ. So
it was with Enos in the Book of Mormon. So it was
with Adam "who made all things known to his sons
and daughters. . . ."

*   *   *

So it was with a young athlete, Gilbert Tobler. He,
too, had a testimony of the gospel and wanted to share
it with others. Gil had been outstanding in sports
throughout his life and had gained wide honors playing defensive football during his years at a university.
Because of his all-around athletic abilities, he was a
valuable person in the eyes of professional sports
leaders.

A football coach from the Detroit Lions visited
the area and made Gil an offer. Gil declined the attractive offer because he had received a call to fulfil a
mission and he wanted to accept that call. When the
coach returned to his ball club, the manager couldn't
believe that such an offer had been declined. The
team's public relations man was then sent to see Gil.
This time the offer was made even more attractive.
The Detroit Lions promised to arrange his playing
schedule so that during the off-seasons he could attend
medical school, which he very much wanted to do. Gil
again declined this enticing offer without hesitation.
The invitation wasn't even tempting to him. He knew
that before medical school, there was to be a mission
in his life. He explained his decision to the man from
the Detroit Lions by taking him to Temple Square in
Salt Lake City.

Gil was also notified that he had been accepted by a
medical school. The dean told him that if he didn't
enter the school at that time but instead went on his

mission, he would never be accepted again. This could have discouraged Gil because it was his great ambition to become a doctor, but it didn't. It was his most pressing desire to fulfil a mission. He felt that both a mission and medical school were possible. He knew that if he served the Lord, all things would work out.

Gil left for his mission field and completed a very honorable and successful mission in South Africa.

Upon his return, he found that during his absence a new dean had been appointed over the medical school. Gil applied again and was accepted. He completed his medical schooling and pursued training as a specialist. Throughout his training, the way seemed to be prepared for him, and he and his wife and children were abundantly blessed. Now Dr. Gilbert Tobler is a successful practising orthopedic surgeon. His life, and that of others who have made similar decisions, is a testimony to us of the word of the Lord when he said, "I, the Lord, am bound when ye do what I say. . . . "

*   *   *

Parents can do a great deal towards having their sons or daughters fulfil missions by:

1. Teaching them about the gospel and helping them gain a testimony so they will *want* to fulfil missions.

2. Talking about "When you go on a mission . . ." rather than "if you go on a mission . . ." and including in family prayers thoughts about a future mission.

3. Encouraging them to prepare themselves by putting part of their money in a mission fund

studying the gospel

studying a foreign language at school (even if that particular language is never used in the mission field, just the fact that one studied a foreign language can help him learn another language easier. It can even help one speak better English!)

planning in advance so that their schooling and tour of duty with the armed services can be correlated with their missions

keeping physically well and morally clean.

4. Devoting occasional family home evenings or dinner table discussions to stories about missionary work and experiences.

5. Discussing nations of the world—their history, culture, and people. (Even if the mission call is to one's neighboring state, any knowledge of other people helps one to be more tolerant, understanding, and loving.)

Family Activities

We remember 10% of what we read;
We remember 20% of what we see;
We remember 50% of what we read and see;
We remember 90% of what we do.

Our Father in heaven has said, ". . . this is my work and my glory—to bring to pass the immortality and eternal life of man." (Moses 1:39.) To accomplish this great purpose, he has placed us here on earth to let us work out our own salvation. He will do nothing for us that we can do for ourselves because he knows that our individual development and progress depend upon our experiencing and *doing* things for ourselves.

As earthly parents, we, too, are deeply concerned about the immortality and eternal life of our children. It is our sacred obligation to set the stage so that they might experience and do the things which will help bring about their eventual exaltation. In conducting weekly family home evenings, the more children actually *do*, the more they will remember, and consequently the more they will be able to apply in their lives.

PLANNING, PREPARING, TAKING PART

Family home evenings can be doubly effective if the children take turns actually planning and conducting them, under the direction of the father who should preside. Older children, who might be inclined toward boredom, could have tremendous experiences preparing and teaching some of the lessons. Not only does this alleviate the boredom, but it really develops these grown children because the teacher always learns the most!

Young children can recite poems, tell stories, and give short talks along with the regular weekly family home evening lessons. Our young children love to present lessons which they have prepared all on their own. We are constantly amazed by their creative abilities as they use visual materials, "attention getters," and original stories. What these little lessons may lack in continuity sometimes is well compensated by what the children gain in real growth and development. One lesson given is worth several lessons heard!

Older children can be assigned book or article reviews from church or other worthwhile publications; for instance, a teenager could read the current issue of *The New Era* and then report on the article which impressed him most.

Tremendous growth on the part of children can be realized by having them regularly give talks as a part of your family home evening. Children may either select their own subjects or on occasion the parents might assign a subject to which they should speak.

Once in a while it can be challenging and worthwhile to call on a child for an impromptu talk. You might say, "Steve, will you please stand and talk to us for two minutes about the Word of Wisdom," or "Ann, would you please take several minutes to tell us what the ideal of temple marriage means to you," or "Beth, would you please give a short talk on the significance of prayer." Such an activity helps teach children to think on their feet, it helps parents to know how their children really feel, and certainly no one is ever bored!

HOMEMADE TELEVISION PROGRAMS OR FILMSTRIPS

A "television program" or "filmstrip" offers a unique family activity. Illustrations and a script, if desired, should be pasted on a roll of paper, and then the roll of paper is to be inserted in a pasteboard box so that it can be viewed by the audience of family members as it is rolled. Following is a sample script with illustrations:

A Special Little Penny

In the child's outstretched hand
The pennies waited eagerly,
Wondering what he'd do with them
And what their future tasks would be.
At first there were ten pennies,
Then suddenly just nine,
For the child had taken one and said
"Little penny, you're not mine.
You're a very special penny
With a special job to do.
You're the brightest, shiniest one of all
That's why I've chosen you.
Each time I get ten pennies
One must be returned
To my Heavenly Father to do his work,
For the law of tithing I have learned.
I have so many blessings
And such a grateful heart
And even though one cent is small
I'm glad to do my part.
So I'll put you in my tithing box
And you must patient be,
Till Sunday when I'll take you out
To go to church with me."
While the little penny waited,
He thought of his job with pride
And promised to do the best he could.
He felt happy and good inside.

Then Sunday came, and to church he went
Clutched in the child's hand
And was given to the bishop
Just as the child had planned.
But now the little penny
Was no longer all alone;
There were many others also
Sharing his new home.

BISHOP

Not only were there pennies
But nickels, dimes as well,
And many, many dollars—
Just how many he couldn't tell.
"What are you all doing here?"
The little penny asked;
"Are you ordinary money
Or do you, too, have a special task?"

Then an older, wiser, nickel said,
"We're special, just like you,
For we're all tithing money
With important jobs to do."
"I know that tithing money
Belongs unto the Lord,
And that those who pay their tithing
Will receive a rich reward.
But just exactly what's my job?
In what way can I work?
I want to know just what to do,
For I don't want to shirk."

"We'll tell you," said the others,
And they smiled at the penny,
"For there is much work to be done
And the helpers must be many.
Temples and chapels must be built
In which church members can meet.
So we must do whatever we can
To make this work complete.
The missionary program
Which brings eternal joy
Is helped by tithing pennies
From every girl and boy.
Seminaries, institutes,
And schools in foreign lands,
Are just another worthy cause

Where we must lend a hand.
There are still more places
Where we can be of service,
The wondrous genealogy
Is a program that deserves us.
At conference time and other times
Throughout the world we go
Bringing people inspiration
Through TV and radio.
The leaders of the Church
With much traveling to do
To visit Saints throughout the world
Need help from me and you.
Then there are many other things
In which we do a share.
You can see just how important
We are to people everywhere."
"My goodness," said the penny,
"I am so very small,
And there's so much work that should be done;
Am I any good at all?"
"Oh, yes," sang all the others.
"If we don't work as one,
We could never even start
On all that must be done.
That's why every single penny
Is as important as can be
In carrying out the work of God
To help build eternity."
So the shiny, happy penny
Was sent with the nickels and dimes
To the headquarters of the Church
To join others from all the climes.
Together they're working diligently
To fulfill a marvelous plan,
For tithing is part of the Lord's special way
To bring happiness and blessing to man.

MUSICAL EVENINGS

Musical renditions on the part of family members

can be coordinated with regular family home evenings to the enjoyment and edification of everyone.

Singing together as a family is delightful and helps to establish an atmosphere of love and happiness. Our two-year-old daughter likes this time best of all because she "leads" the singing. This is one way even a very young child can learn to participate.

DRAMATIZATIONS.
PANTOMIMES, CHARADES

Simple dramatizations with the family members forming the cast can impress a lesson on the minds of children. A number of the stories in the *Church Family Home Evening Manual* could be adapted as dramatizations. Incidents from the Bible, Book of Mormon, or church history easily lend themselves to dramatizations.

Pantomimes are simple, yet they can be very effective. Each Christmas Eve at our traditional family get-together, our children along with their little cousins pantomime the story of the First Christmas. The parts of Mary and Joseph are rotated among the children from year to year, and a favorite doll or a newborn baby plays the part of baby Jesus. Robes, scarves, and towels bedeck the other children out as the shepherds and wisemen. It seems that even the littlest shepherd is able to stand still while an older child reads the story of the First Christmas from the Gospel of Luke. Then everyone joins in singing "Away in a Manger."

Charades is a game whereby the audience attempts to guess a story or incident as the actors dramatize or depict in some way the meaning of each word in the title. Playing charades is another way to make a lesson memorable.

MEMORIES EVENING

To help build vivid memories and correct values in the minds of children of what things in life are most precious and important, a memories evening could be held occasionally. Family albums and record books could be enjoyed or family slides or movies could be viewed. New pictures might be taken. Tape recordings could be reviewed and perhaps a new tape could be made. Memories of special events connected with family trips and outings could be recalled. An additional highlight to the evening could be having each person present express what his choicest experience of the year has been.

THIS IS YOUR LIFE!

A very special way to spend an activity night would be to have a "This Is Your Life" program. This program could be planned for a member of the family whose birthday comes during the month or for mother on Mother's Day or for father on Father's Day or as a special surprise to grandparents.

Stories and pictures from the honored person's life, prepared and presented by family members, offer an ideal way to carry out this program.

Plan to sing the favorite songs of the honored person and be sure to serve some of his favorite food!

SPECIAL GUESTS

A young boy received a bicycle for his sixth birthday. Before his parents gave him the bike, however, they invited a policeman friend (in full uniform) to visit one of their family home evenings. He talked to the children about bicycle safety and other safety rules pertinent to them. These rules coming directly from this friendly policeman were much more impressive and helpful than anything parents could say.

A fireman could be invited in to talk about fire safety and how to work with matches and campfires.

Some children never have the privilege of seeing a returned missionary much closer than from where they sit in church to the pulpit. Lasting values could be gleaned by inviting an outstanding, enthusiastic returned missionary to your home to talk to your children. His spirit and enthusiasm could be a great motivating factor in helping a young child live worthy of a mission.

FAMILY FIX-IT NIGHT

Projects can provide great times. A family "fix-it night" when the mother and girls mend and the father and sons handle any maintenance work and repair jobs is fun as well as helpful. This activity, as well as any other, should be crowned with a freezer of homemade ice cream, freshly popped corn, root beer floats, or some other treat.

DISPLAYS

Let the family show off their creative abilities. If you have a place in your home for a bulletin board, a table or mirror in the living room, or any other appropriate place, the children would love making different types of displays for these areas. They can use holiday or seasonal themes, or perhaps they can illustrate an important gospel teaching or something you are currently emphasizing in your family home evenings. Turn them loose with crepe paper, construction paper, pictures, and all kinds of odds and ends. You might be surprised what they can come up with!

BUZZ SESSIONS

It might be effective to hold occasional buzz sessions during your lessons or when discussing a family problem. Divide the family into at least two groups and allow them a few minutes to discuss the problem and exchange ideas. Then have one member from each group summarize the discussion and report to the entire family.

QUESTION BOX

A question box can take just part of the evening or occasionally take the entire lesson period. Let family members know in advance when you will be using the question box so they can put any questions they want in it. You may limit the questions to one particular subject or open it to questions in any category. Then the family may answer these questions together, assign just one member to answer, or even have a special visitor come in to answer questions some evening. The question box can also be used as a game by putting in questions regarding recent family night lessons or gospel subjects and letting family members take turns drawing questions and answering them.

WHAT ARE FAMILIES FOR?

Children need to learn early in life how they fit into their family and what is expected of them. Some children grow up feeling that their parents should be their slaves, doing anything and everything the child desires. Other children may grow up feeling they carry an unfair share of the family responsibility and fail to realize the many things their parents are doing in their behalf.

It is important to teach our children that each family member has responsibilities and contributions to make to the family and that even though each may contribute something entirely different, the family cannot operate successfully unless we all do our fair share. If this lesson were honestly learned it might solve many family problems!

In teaching a lesson on this subject, why not bake a family cake? Let each member of the family represent one or more ingredients and then let each one contribute the ingredient he is representing. Make sure the children understand that the cake would fail if even one thing were left out or if one ingredient were too lazy to do the job you expected of it. (Another approach —although it would ruin a good cake—is to leave out one ingredient and really show the children what would happen!)

Family Cake Recipe:

2 cups flour	This would be father—the sturdy foundation upon which the whole family is built.
1½ cups sugar	Mother would be the sugar—adding the right touch of sweetness to the home.
1 teaspoon salt	Little Tim would be the salt—what a flop our cake would be without this much-needed touch.
2 teaspoons baking powder	Big sister Sharon can be the baking powder — this family wouldn't get far without her willing and capable help.
Sift dry ingredients three times and add: ½ cup margarine, butter, or oil	Bob would be the butter—his sense of humor and agreeable personality add richness to our family life.

1 cup milk	Ellen is the milk—she is able to combine the abilities of the rest of the family by being where she is needed most at just the right time.
1 teaspoon vanilla	This would be baby Steven—he is still so small but gives our family a delicious flavor.
Blend and then beat in: Two large eggs	What would we do without the eggs?!—or without our Linda. Many of our activities would fall flat, just like the cake, without her pep and enthusiasm.
Mix 2 to 3 minutes	Now the ingredients must be blended so that you can't distinguish one from the other—alone they are not much good! Only when they are combined, do they become something special.

Now bake the cake in the oven of the gospel (at 375 degrees for 25-30 minutes) to make it rise to perfection and ice it with the sweetness of love.

GOALS

Sometimes people waste many years of their lives because they are not quite sure in which direction they should go. We, as Latter-day Saints, should never have this problem. The Lord has revealed to us through his prophets just what the purpose of our life on earth should be. Children should understand this early in life so that they know where they are headed. They should set for themselves many goals—some small, some great, some short-range and some long-range goals—all of which should eventually lead them to the all-important goal of eternal exaltation.

It would be helpful, then, to do something with your children that will make them stop and think about what is really important and what they want out of life. One method in which this could be accomplished is through the following family activity.

Write a short biography of each family member, making an effort to include incidents they have especially enjoyed as well as their accomplishments in life so far. Then give each family member his own story to finish. (This activity is especially good for older children, but even small children would enjoy having someone else help them write theirs.) Have each one write his story just the way he hopes it will happen. Have him include school and school activities (you may discover that your small daughter has her heart set on becoming a cheerleader in high school or that your son thinks as much of being a basketball star as he does of going on a mission!), the part the Church should play in his life, a mission, when and where he would like to marry, what occupation he is interested in, etc.

Emphasize that it is his power to make this story come true! It might be a good idea to file the completed biography in a place where the child can read it occasionally so he can compare his real life with the one he hopes to have.

Following is a sample biography:

Once upon a time not too many years ago, a very special little blond-haired, blue-eyed baby was born. Right from the first this was a happy little girl because she had parents, grandparents, relatives, and friends who loved her and took care of her. When she was still just a little baby, she learned how to crawl. Her mother remembers the very first Christmas after she was born. She was only five months old, yet she was able to get into all the Christmas presents and pull the icicles off the bottom branches of the Christmas tree. From that time on she got into all kinds of mischief, but her mother and father didn't mind too much because they knew that's how babies learn things. Do you know who this baby was? Yes, of course it was *you!*

Little by little you grew up. You got teeth, learned to walk and run and play games, learned to feed yourself, and most important of all began to learn what you could and couldn't do. When you were two a baby sister was born, and even though you were still quite small, you helped take care of her, and you loved to play with her.

When you were old enough, you started going to Junior Sunday School and Primary, and we were so proud of you when the teachers told us what a good girl you were. You listened quietly and liked to answer the questions, and you always did what the teachers asked. You loved to go to church!

At home you were a little ray of sunshine. Sometimes you were naughty, but most of the time you tried very hard to do what was right. You have a voice like a little angel, and everyone loves to hear you sing. You are a lovely little dancer also and have started learning to play the piano. You have made everyone happy with your music.

A little baby brother was born, and by this time you were big enough to feed and tend him. Then, too, you were old enough to be a good helper at home because you had learned to do dishes, dust, vacuum, and other things. Do you remember the summers you went to nursery school, and at home how you started learning to read, do arithmetic, and tell time?

Before long you started going to school. A whole wonderful new world opened up to you there! So much to learn, so much to do, and so many new friends! You worked hard and played hard at school—so of course you have enjoyed it.

When you were eight, a very important event took place. You were baptized and confirmed a member of the Church. Bishop White talked to you about your baptism and what it meant, and also the responsibility that came with it. Your grandparents traveled many miles just to share this wonderful occasion with you, and we had a lovely dinner with the family to honor you.

Now you are even older and have many other important things to look forward to. The future years of your life hold many treasures in store for you. What would you like them to be?

TESTIMONY HOUR

One of the most impressive and valuable of any family home evening activity has been our monthly testimony time.

Suggested approach: lesson and group activity

A little girl asked her mother what the word "believe" meant. The mother defined it as best she could. Finally the little girl looked up with understanding on her face and said, "Oh, I see! To believe is to hear in my heart."

*   *   *

A testimony is a feeling in your heart to help you believe the gospel is true. A testimony is also a feeling of thankfulness for blessings received from our Heavenly Father. Frequently when people bear (or say) their testimonies, they tell a personal experience (or story) about something which helped them to have a stronger belief about the gospel or they express their thankfulness for a certain blessing.

Testimonies are so important to us that once each month in the Church we have a special meeting just for people to bear their testimonies. This meeting is on fast Sunday and it is called fast meeting. Anyone in the ward who would like to may stand up and bear his testimony (or express thankfulness for the Church and his blessings). It is wonderful to have this opportunity to bear our testimonies and to hear other members of the Church bear theirs. Fast meeting is one of our very favorite meetings.

Very often when people give 2½ minute talks in Sunday School or speak in Sacrament meeting, they bear their testimonies as part of their talk. Next time you hear someone speak, listen closely for his testimony.

Missionaries who preach the gospel to people who are not members of the Church frequently bear their testimonies to them. This helps those people to gain testimonies of their own and to want to become members of the Church.

Sometimes on special occasions in the family we bear our testimonies. We do this during our family prayers. At Christmas and Thanksgiving time or on birthdays we sometimes bear our testimonies to each other. During our family hours would be another good time to bear our testimonies.

Let's make this family hour tonight a very special one and bear our testimonies to each other. (Review briefly what a testimony is and in general what could be said.) Mother and Father and all family members who desire to do so may take turns bearing testimonies.

SABBATH DAY

Suggested approach: lesson and group activity
Materials needed: scrapbook, magazines (that can
   be cut up), scissors, paste.

A little boy received a red wagon for his birthday.
For days he went nowhere without it. But there came
an afternoon when he was happily pulling it along
the front sidewalk, and his father said: "Take that
wagon in back and play with it. Don't you know it
is Sunday?"

The boy started to obey and then stopped, turned
around and faced his father with a puzzled look. "Isn't
it Sunday in the back yard, too?" he asked.

* * *

Our Heavenly Father has asked us to rest from
our work and have a very special day each Sunday or
Sabbath day. Daddy stays home from work, and
Mother doesn't clean the house or wash or iron or
shop. (We have noticed that example plays a tremendous part right here. Our children play differently
with their dolls on Sunday. Instead of playing house
and ironing and sweeping, they dress their dolls for
church and play Sunday School.)

Sunday is a wonderful day. We go to Sunday
School and Sacrament meeting, have our Family Hour
and do things which help us to feel closer to our Heavenly Father. At our home we find that three little
rules help us to keep the Sabbath day holy:

1. We spend no money.
2. We stay dressed in our Sunday clothes.
3. We do things which help us feel closer to our
   Father in heaven.

This evening for our Family Hour activity, let us go through these magazines and cut out pictures of things which would be good to do on the Sabbath day. Then we can paste the pictures in this scrapbook. From now on when we wonder what we can do on Sunday, we need only to look through our scrapbook to find lots of good ideas for Sabbath activities.

(Suggestions for things to do, to be pasted in the scrapbook, could be: visiting people who need cheering, letter writing, drawing pictures of Sunday School lesson, working on scrapbooks and Books of Remembrance, listening to good music, reading and telling stories in keeping with spirit of day, preparing talks for church, playing quiet, appropriate games, putting jig-saw puzzles together.)

THOUGHTFULNESS

Suggested approach: Pixie Game (family activity)

Materials needed: slips of paper containing names of family members

The Pixie Game is delightful for children of all ages.   The object of the game is to do as many kind deeds for someone as possible without letting him discover who his "pixie" is.   Some families have enjoyed this game so much they have made it a tradition to have one pixie week each year.

Let each person draw a slip of paper containing another family member's name.   He will then play pixie for the entire week to that person by doing as many kind and fun things as possible.   Of course, each pixie tries his best to keep his identity a secret until the end of the week when it is revealed through an especially kind deed or small gift.   Fun or complimentary notes and poems can accompany each surprise, and the best way to keep everyone guessing as to who his pixie is, is to do kind deeds for other family members, too.

During this week the children will truly experience the joy that comes in doing good to others.

See who can do the most kind things without being discovered!

Suggested activities the pixies can secretly do for the person they are assigned to, are:

do his chores
shine his shoes
make his bed
play his favorite record
put a special surprise under his pillow
leave a bedtime snack by his bed at night
arrange to have his favorite menu for dinner
put a nice treat in his lunchbox
let him watch his favorite TV program
never complain or argue with him
always be alert to anything that will bring him
    enjoyment

Gospel Lessons

PRAYER

Suggested approach: flannelboard demonstration

Materials needed: pictures illustrating the four steps
to prayer

(For lessons adapted to older children, see Puzzle
Piece IV for stories on prayer.)

Young children pray more willingly and express
themselves more effectively when they really are
taught how to pray. We have found this simple flannelboard lesson helpful. (Sometimes we, as parents,
take the lead of the lesson and the children offer suggestions for things for which they are grateful and
for blessings they would like. Other times we let a
child—each one gets a turn eventually—present the
entire lesson to the family, using the flannelboard pictures available. This latter method is most successful
because it is the teacher who always learns the most!
Frequently the entire lesson is repeated by the children in their prayers that evening.)

Did you know that there are four steps to a
prayer? We pray to our Father in heaven, so the first
thing we say is: *Our Father in heaven* (phrase put on
flannelboard). Little boys pray (picture of young boy
praying is placed on flannelboard), little girls pray
(similar picture of girl is placed on board), big boys
and girls pray, mothers and daddies pray, grand-

mothers and grandfathers pray—*everyone prays.* (Appropriate pictures used to illustrate latter points also.)

Then after saying, "Our Father in heaven," the second thing we do is say *we thank thee* (word strip placed on board) for our blessings. As blessings are enumerated, corresponding pictures (cut from magazines and other sources) are placed on board. Example: We're thankful for a mother who reads us stories, for a daddy who plays with us, for our family who love one another and have happy times together, for our lovely home, for our good food, for our teachers at church and school, for the friendly policeman who helps us cross a busy street on our way to school, for our friends. . . .

After we have expressed our thankfulness, then the third step is *we ask thee* (word strip placed on flannelboard) to help us and to bless us. Again appropriate pictures are used to illustrate such things as: Help us to be obedient and do what is right, help us to help each other and Mother and Daddy, help us to do our best in school. We ask thee to bless our loved ones; we ask thee to bless the missionaries who are preaching the gospel. . . .

Then, we close our prayer by saying, *in the name of Jesus Christ. Amen.* (word strip placed on flannelboard). Jesus Christ (place picture of Savior on flannelboard) has told us that we are to pray in his name. Then everyone present says "Amen" which means that we are all in agreement with the things said in the prayer.

Each time we pray, let us try to remember these four steps. What are they again? Review.

WHAT DO YOU SAY?—HOW DO YOU SAY IT?

Suggested approach: family members assume various characterizations and dramatize the parts. Make certain that eventually everyone has a turn to be Prepared Polly or Parry. Then several (or all) family members could present talks, following the points of a good speech. Constructive criticism by others in the family could be helpful in teaching children how to speak effectively. (Following this lesson are several sample talks which suggest the type of talk a young person might give.)

Bashful Betty: This young lady talks in such a tiny little voice and ducks her head so, that we miss most of what she has to say. We are sorry she is so frightened. We hope you are never a Bashful Betty.

Wandering Willie: He sounds as though he is far away from home and lost without a compass or roadmap. He wanders back and forth and jumps from here to there so that it makes us tired just to listen. You would never be a Wandering Willie.

Bookish Bobby: His talks sound as though he has copied them from some grown-up's book. Sometimes he can't even pronounce all the words! It's obvious that he isn't understanding a thing he is reading, and neither are we. Thank goodness you're not a Bookish Bobby.

Five Minute Freddie: While listening to him speak, we strongly suspect that his preparing was done about the last five minutes. You certainly aren't a Five Minute Freddie, are you.

Mumbling Millie: This young lady talks as though she were still eating her breakfast oatmeal. Try as we do, it is practically impossible to understand her. She isn't popular at all. We hope you will never be like her.

Reader Rudy: All we can see of this speaker is the top of his head, and his voice sounds like something from a talking machine. It is difficult to be interested in a talk which is read. You will never read a talk, will you.

Ever-Ending Eddie: This young man has been heard to close his talk five times before he actually stops speaking and sits down. He is a trial to everyone who is listening. You surely aren't an Ever-Ending Eddie.

* * *

Prepared Polly: She is a joy to all of us. Because she is prepared, she feels confident rather than bashful. Her talk has an interesting beginning, and she knows where she is going and when to stop; she never wanders a bit! She, with the help of her parents, has developed some thoughts which are meaningful to her and to those who listen as well; she reads good books and learns from them, but she doesn't copy them. She is such a good speaker that anyone can tell her talks weren't made up at the last minute. She is so enthusiastic about the message she is presenting that she speaks each word clearly and distinctly so everyone can understand her. Because she is Prepared Polly, she never, never would read her talk. She presents her message so well it sounds as though she has practised it before family members or the bedroom mirror. As soon as her point has been made, she ends her speech with a challenging thought and sits down. Isn't Prepared Polly wonderful! We hope you will always be a Prepared Polly—or Parry!

TALK FOR A YOUNG CHILD
(3 to 5 years)

JOSEPH SMITH STORY

One time there was a boy named Joseph Smith, and he wondered which church to join. His mother and daddy and brothers and sisters went to different churches, and he wondered which church was the right one. One day he went to the woods and prayed to Heavenly Father and a very wonderful thing happened. Heavenly Father and Jesus came and talked to Joseph Smith and told him that he should join none of the churches because not one of them was the right one. Heavenly Father and Jesus told Joseph Smith that if he would keep on being a good boy that some day he could help them organize the right church. Joseph Smith was a good boy and helped Heavenly Father and Jesus put the right church on the earth. The name of it is The Church of Jesus Christ of Latter-day Saints.

I am thankful to be a little Latter-day Saint boy. (girl). I say this in the name of Jesus Christ. Amen.

TALK FOR A CHILD
(6 to 8 years old)

KING DAVID

One time the Lord told the Prophet Samuel to go to Bethlehem to perform a special mission. Samuel was to help choose a king and the Lord told him to go to the home of a man named Jesse and there he would find the person who was to be the new king.

Samuel was to take his horn of oil and anoint the head of the man who was chosen to be king. He went to the house of Jesse and told him that one of his sons was to be chosen king of Israel.

Jesse had many fine sons, so he called the eldest in for Samuel to see. This boy was so tall and noble looking that Samuel thought, "Surely this young man must be the one whom God has chosen." But the Lord said, "No, Samuel, he is not the one." Then came another son, another tall, handsome, well-dressed lad. Samuel took up his horn of oil to anoint him, but again the Lord said, "No, no, not this one, Samuel, for I have not chosen him."

One by one the sons of Jesse came to Samuel and each time Samuel thought that surely this must be the one who was to be the new king of Israel and each time the Lord would say: "No, no, Samuel, I have not chosen him."

Finally Jesse said, "You are not looking for one of my sons, Samuel." And then Samuel asked, "Have you no other sons?" Jesse said, "Yes, one other. My little boy David. He is out herding the sheep."

The prophet said, "Send for David."

Finally David arrived and Samuel was surprised to see that he was a boy just fifteen years of age. He was not dressed well like his brothers; his feet were bare and he had on ordinary shepherd's clothes.

The Lord said to the prophet, "Take your horn of oil, Samuel, and anoint him King of Israel, for I, the Lord, have selected him." And then the Lord said, "Remember, men look upon the outward appearance but God looketh upon the heart."

And so David, the shepherd boy, became king, and God talked with him and showed David how to be kind and good. David played upon the harp and made lovely music, too, and sang songs about the goodness of God to his people.

This is one of the loveliest of David's songs:

The Lord is my shepherd; I shall not want.
He maketh me to lie down in green pastures;
He leadeth me beside the still waters.
He restoreth my soul;
He leadeth me in the paths of righteousness for his name's
    sake.

Yea, though I walk through the valley of the shadow of death,
I will fear no evil: for thou art with me;
Thy rod and thy staff they comfort me.
Thou preparest a table before me in the presence of mine
enemies.
Thou anointest my head with oil; my cup runneth over.
Surely goodness and mercy shall follow me all the days of my
life;
And I will dwell in the house of the Lord forever.

(Psalm 23.)

I pray that when the Lord looks upon our hearts, he will find them pure and that we will always live so the Lord may be our Shepherd, in the name of Jesus Christ. Amen.

BAPTISM

Lesson to help young children prepare for baptism
Suggested approach: simple explanation of what
takes place in connection with a baptism

Before you can be baptized, you must know about the gospel. Your parents and your Sunday School and Primary teachers have been teaching you.

You must be eight years old. Our Heavenly Father tells us that when a child is eight years old, he is old enough to know right from wrong and can be held responsible or accountable for all that he does.

You must be worthy. Before you can be baptized and become a member of the kingdom of God, you must live your very best every day and keep the commandments of Heavenly Father.

You will plan for your baptism with us. Mother and Daddy will talk to you about where and when you are baptized and what you need to do to be ready.

The bishop of our ward will visit with you about baptism. He will ask you several questions about the gospel and set the date for your baptism.

When the time comes, we will go to the place where you are to be baptized.

You will go to a special dressing room and put on white clothing, which is a sign of cleanliness and purity.

After you are dressed in your white clothing and just before you are baptized, a short meeting will be held for all of those who are going to be baptized. A member of the Church will give a talk about the wonderful thing which is to take place—your baptism.

Then when your name is called, you will go into the water. Daddy (or someone else who holds the priesthood) will help you and show you how to place your hands so no water will go up your nose.

Then you will be immersed (completely covered with water) in the water for just a moment.

After you come up out of the water, you will return to the dressing room and put on your own clothing.

Later, several men holding the priesthood (such as your father, the bishop, and his counselors) will lay their hands upon your head and confirm you a member of The Church of Jesus Christ of Latter-day Saints and say to you "receive the Holy Ghost." (See lesson on baptism, page 190 and the lesson on the Holy Ghost, page 202 for more detailed explanations.)

When you are baptized and are a member of the Church, you will want to stand up during testimony meeting once in a while and bear your testimony as you have done in our family for special Family Hours. (See testimony lesson on page 172.) Perhaps you could bear your testimony on the very day that you are confirmed a member of the Church.

After your baptism, Mother and Daddy want to do something very special in your honor. (Perhaps an outstanding event could be dinner in a restaurant with the parents and children.)

Then after you are confirmed in fast meeting, we want to have a family dinner for you. We will invite Grandmother and Grandfather (perhaps others, too) and you may select your very favorite foods which Mother will prepare and serve. We will have a wonderful time together and make it a memorable occasion for you.

That evening, as you kneel by your bed to pray, you will have a very special blessing for which to thank your Father in heaven. You will want him to know how grateful you are to now be a member of his Church. You will ask him to help you to be a good member always.

LIFE IS A JOURNEY

Baptism

Note to parents: Baptism is one of the four most important things that will occur in one's life. The other three are birth, marriage, and death. When we view baptism in this light, we understand more fully the importance of it and the necessity of making our children feel what a truly special event this is. The purpose of this lesson is to prepare a child for baptism by explaining to him the significance of baptism as the entrance into the kingdom of God and to create in him a desire to make his baptism meaningful in his life.

This lesson, as outlined, is quite long and could be presented for the first time during two or three different family hours. However, before a child is baptized, he should hear it once in its entirety and should be well enough acquainted with the material that he can explain much of it himself. (The flip chart lesson on baptism—previous lesson—should teach a child what to expect on his baptismal day.)

A child should begin anticipating his eighth birthday well in advance of the actual date. He should understand that this birthday is more important than others he has had because he will then be old enough to be baptized. It is essential to have the child baptized as soon as possible after his eighth birthday. To be baptized on his birthday is a wonderful occurrence if the arrangements can be made. Otherwise, he should be baptized during his birthday month.

Following are some ways in which you could make baptism a memorable event for your child:

Let the child attend at least one baptismal service prior to his own so he will understand the procedure and know what to expect. (This helps dispel any fears the child might have.)

Encourage him to invite close friends and relatives to his baptismal service. Make him feel truly important in every way.

Have a special dinner in the child's honor after his baptism. (Some families take the child to dinner in a restaurant after he has been baptized, and then after he has been confirmed a family dinner, with grandparents and other close relatives included, is held in his honor.)

Present him with an appropriate remembrance. One family gives each of their children a copy of the Book of Mormon at this time. On the inside of the cover they paste a snapshot of the child taken after his baptism in front of the building where the service was held.

Suggested approach: The way leading to the kingdom of God compared to the journey of life.

Do you remember the vacation we took last summer? We had a delightful time, didn't we. Can you remember, too, the many things we had to do to get ready for it? Going on a trip takes some preparation if we want to enjoy it and make it successful. For instance, Daddy found a road map before we left so he could select the right roads. Mother helped you pack the clothes you would need in your suitcase. We took a lunch to eat in the car. You chose a book and a game to read and to enjoy as we rode in the car. As we drove along the highway, Daddy watched for road signs so he could keep the car on the right course. When we reached our destination, we had a wonderful time. We were so happy to be there.

We often take trips or journeys during our lifetime. In fact, life itself is a journey. In order to make this journey we need a map which points out the right road which will lead us to our destination. This map is our religion, the gospel of Jesus Christ. If we should ever lose the gospel, it would be much like losing our road map, and we would get lost and waste a lot of time trying to find our way back.

For *this* journey we don't pack a suitcase with clothing. Instead we fill our body with health and strength, place love and a determination to reach our goal in our heart, and fill our mind with knowledge and good thoughts. We have to be careful to follow each road sign along the way. Some of these road signs are teachings that our parents give us, the things we learn at Sunday School and Primary and lessons we learn at school. If we follow the right course, which is the gospel, and do what the road signs tell us to do as we travel along, we will reach our destination which is the kingdom of God in heaven. There we can live in the presence of our Heavenly Father.

Today we are going to talk about this journey of life. In fact, let's pretend that we are taking this trip.

> Here's the map or chart
> we will use to show us ➡
> the steps we must take:

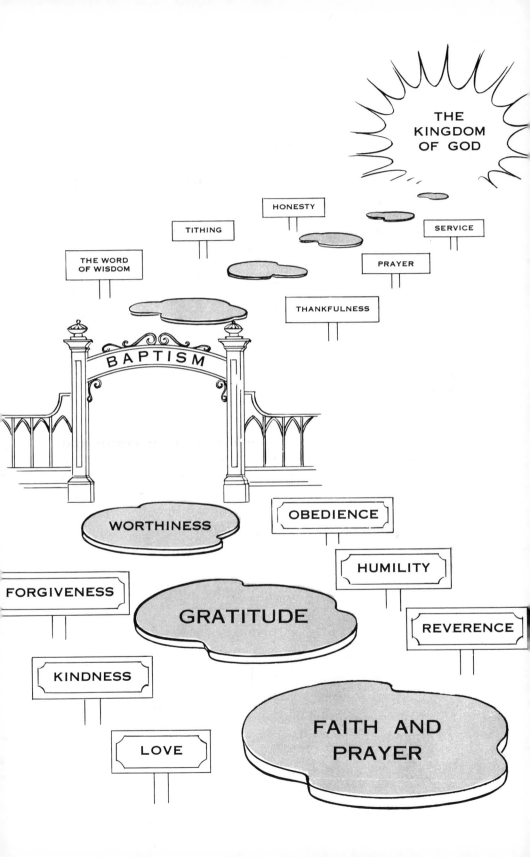

FAITH AND PRAYER (Step one)

You already have faith in your Heavenly Father or you would not desire to be baptized. You know that he loves you and that he wants you to be happy here on earth. It is easy to have faith in Heavenly Father because we see so many things around us to let us know he cares about us. The beautiful earth and everything on it are a constant reminder to us that he is watching over us. He has given us loving parents and wonderful friends. Having faith helps us live a better life because we understand more the importance of the things we do. A farmer plants his seeds each spring, having faith they will grow. A grocer stocks his shelves with food having faith his customers will buy the food. You go to school each morning, having faith your teacher will be there to teach you. We wouldn't do anything in life if we didn't have faith.

The second part of this step is prayer. Our Heavenly Father knows we often need to talk to him about our problems and experiences. We need to ask him for help and guidance. We should express our gratitude to him for the good things in our lives.

If you want to share some good news with a friend or ask his advice, you would probably go see him or call him on the telephone. Or if you want to tell your grandparents something important and they live far away, you might write them a letter. After writing the letter you must put it in an envelope, address it correctly, place a stamp on it, and mail it.

But when we want to talk to our Heavenly Father, we must do it in a very special way—through prayer. Just as the letters you mail must be properly addressed and stamped, so must our prayers be done in the right way. We always bow our head and close our eyes as we talk to our Heavenly Father. We must remember that there are four steps to a good prayer. Since prayer will become even more important to you after your baptism because you will need constant guidance from your Heavenly Father, let us review the four steps to a good prayer.

OUR FATHER IN HEAVEN—we address our prayer to him always.

WE THANK THEE—for our home, parents, sisters and brothers, food to eat, clothes to wear, teachers, friends, health, minds, happiness, and love we have in our hearts.

WE ASK THEE—to help us, bless those we love (name them), those who are sick, help us to be good and kind.

IN THE NAME OF JESUS CHRIST. AMEN.

If we pray with love in our heart for Heavenly Father and those about us, our Father in heaven will hear our prayers. You know there are different ways of answering a prayer, and through our faith we must learn to recognize and accept every answer. Sometimes the answer may come slowly. Sometimes it may even be no. Often it will just be the opportunity for you to earn the blessing. Our Father in heaven loves you and will answer your prayers in the way which will help you the most.

GRATITUDE (Step two)

One of the greatest lessons of life is to learn the value of gratitude or thankfulness. Therefore, the next step on our chart is that of gratitude. Our Father in heaven has given us so many things for which to be grateful. You have a mother who teaches you each day through her words, actions, and kindness. He also gave you a loving father who works hard to give you plenty of wholesome food, nice clothes to wear, and a comfortable home to live in. And besides all of this you have the lovely things of nature—the beautiful flowers, the green grass, the warm sunshine—to help you enjoy your life here and keep you happy.

But most important of all, you should feel grateful for the honor and privilege you have of becoming a member of the Church of Jesus Christ. We know this is the same Church that Christ had when he was on the earth. Because of the restoration of the gospel through Joseph Smith, men in the Church today also have the authority to baptize, just as they did in the days of Christ. This is a tremendous thing we have to be grateful for—that we can be baptized into the Church by men who have the Holy Priesthood. From our membership we are given many opportunities to grow and develop ourselves and serve others so that someday we may be worthy of exaltation in the kingdom of God.

To express our gratitude for all the blessings our Father in heaven has given us, we must live the way he asks us to and express appreciation to him in our prayers each day.

WORTHINESS (Step three)

The next step on our chart is worthiness. We must be worthy of this wonderful blessing of baptism. We can be worthy by doing our very best always, by trying to do what is right. Let me tell you a story about Kristine. After hearing the story, see if you think Kristine was worthy of the blessing she received.

Once there was a lovely little girl whose name was Kristine. She was very excited one certain day because she was getting ready to attend Aunt Valarie's party. Kristine thought this was always the nicest event of the whole year because Aunt Valarie gave very special and wonderful parties. How she had looked forward to the party tonight!

Kristine had carefully washed her face and brushed her hair until it was shining and bright. She was just ready to slip into her prettiest dress when the telephone rang. Soon after, her mother came into Kristine's room looking very concerned. "Kristine," she said, "that phone call was about grandmother. She has fallen and hurt herself and needs me there to help her. I know how much you have looked forward to Aunt Valarie's party, but I have to ask you to stay home to tend the younger children for me. I am so sorry about it, Kristine. But you know how much grandmother needs me right now."

Kristine almost cried she was so disappointed, but she knew she must help out in this emergency. She loved her grandmother and felt terribly sad to know she had had an accident. Kristine told her mother not to worry about the younger children; she would gladly stay home to help.

Kristine had dreamed for months about the party—and there was one very special wish she had thought about. Aunt Valarie had a magnificent jeweled necklace, and each year she selected one girl to have the honor of wearing it at the party. Kristine had so hoped that this year she would be chosen to wear the gorgeous necklace.

Kristine had fallen asleep by the time her mother had returned home. Can you guess what she had been dreaming about while she was asleep? The necklace, of course! When she awoke she found her mother calling her and smiling at her.

Just then the doorbell rang. It was Mr. Darius, Aunt Valarie's chauffeur. He had a package for Kristine. A moment later Kristine was untying a pink satin bow and removing silver paper, saying as she worked, "Isn't it just like Aunt Valarie to do something like this? She's always doing nice things for people. What do you suppose it is?"

"Probably some of her little frosted cakes," smiled Mother.

"I hope so," Kristine replied. "Anyway, we'll soon know. Here comes the lid!" But it was not cakes that met Kristine's eyes. There in a nest of crinkled tissue paper lay the necklace. Kristine could not believe her eyes. The necklace! Aunt

Valarie's beautiful necklace! Kristine took it from the box. She held it up, watching the jewels sparkle as they caught the light.   Then, as though in a dream, she walked to the mirror, and Mother placed it around her neck.

"Isn't it perfectly lovely!" she breathed as with starlit eyes she looked in the mirror.   "But why did Aunt Valarie give it to me?"

"Perhaps if you read the card you'll know, dear," her mother answered.

Drawing the card from the envelope, Kristine read:

Dear Kristine,

For a long time now I've wondered to whom I should give "the necklace." As you know, it belonged to my grandmother. When I was twelve, just your age, she gave it to me and told me that some day I was to give it to my little girl. Not having a little girl of my own, I wanted to give it to someone who I felt deserved it. Though I've thought of several little girls, I've never been quite sure.   Tonight, however, when Mr. Darius told me what you have done, I was sure. I knew you were the sweet, helpful, loving little girl I always thought you to be and I wanted you to have "the necklace."

I give it to you with love,
Aunt Valarie

When Kristine finished reading, the room seemed very still. Two shimmering tears trembled in her eyes, then she said softly, "Mother, I'm not half as good as Aunt Valarie thinks. I don't really deserve this beautiful gift, but I'm going to try to. I'm going to truly try." And as Kristine turned again to see herself in the mirror, she looked as lovely as the Kristine of her dreams.

Adapted from a story by
Thelma J. Harrison
The Children's Friend
February 1953, pages 80-81

Just as Kristine in the story, our Heavenly Father wants you to truly try to be worthy of the blessings you receive.

BAPTISM   (Step four—gate)

These steps, faith and prayer, gratitude, and worthiness, have led you along in your journey until now you are approaching the gate which leads to our Father in heaven and Jesus Christ. Going through this gate—or being baptized—is one of the very most important things that can ever happen to you. Before you are baptized, it is necessary for you to understand what a wonderful event it is. You are being baptized for two reasons. First, so that you may become a member of The Church of Jesus Christ of Latter-day Saints. Being a member of his Church is a wonderful blessing, but it is also a tremendous responsibility. Whenever we join any important group, there are requirements we must follow.

A little boy named Tommy had many friends that he enjoyed playing with and he was very happy. One day, though, his friends decided it would be fun to have a tunnel club. They made plans to dig a lot of tunnels in the sand to play in. Tommy thought it would be fun to play in the tunnels, and he wanted to be a member of this club. The only thing was, Tommy didn't like to dig tunnels. He just wanted to play in them after the other boys had dug them.

Do you think Tommy should be allowed to join the tunnel club? Of course not. The other boys didn't think he should be a member either until he could learn to take his share of the responsibility and fulfil the requirements.

There are requirements at home you must fulfil in order to contribute to the happiness of your family. At school you have to study in order to get good grades. In fact, we can't belong to any group or organization unless we do the things they require us to do. And so, if we want to be a member of the kingdom of God, there are certain requirements we have to meet.

You must first decide you want to be baptized because of your faith in Jesus Christ and Heavenly Father. You must then promise yourself and your Father in heaven that you will try to do good things always. When you do make mistakes, you must repent of them so that they will never occur again. Then you can be baptized, just as Jesus Christ was baptized by John the Baptist many centuries ago.

When you are baptized, you show the whole world that you have chosen to follow Jesus Christ and his teachings. You say to everyone, through your baptism, that you intend to do only the things that our Savior wants you to and that you will never go against his wishes. As you are baptized, you make a covenant or a promise to your Heavenly Father to serve him always. You must always remember this agreement which you will make at the time you are baptized.

Do you see now what an important step baptism is? After you have been baptized, you will truly be a member of The Church of Jesus Christ of Latter-day Saints.

The second reason it is important for you to be baptized is so that you can receive the gift of the Holy Ghost. After your baptism, men holding the priesthood will lay their hands upon your head to confirm you a member of the Church and then they will say, "receive the Holy Ghost." It is the most special gift your Father in heaven could give you. We pray you will appreciate it and use it as you should. Before you become eight years of age, you are not accountable or responsible for the things you do. When you turn eight, however, our Father in heaven says that you are old enough to be accountable for your actions. Because our Heavenly Father loves you so dearly, he wants you to do the right thing so that you can stay on the right path and some day return to him. He has promised you the gift of the Holy Ghost to guide you and help you to follow the gospel path. This is such an important blessing, that we are going to spend an entire evening very soon discussing the gift of the Holy Ghost. (See following lesson.)

On the day you are baptized, we want you to remember the two reasons why you are being baptized. Can you tell me? That is right. First, to become a member of the Church of Jesus Christ; second, to receive the gift of the Holy Ghost! We are so grateful and proud that you will soon be able to enjoy these blessings.

Each time you attend church, be certain to think of these two reasons and your promise to Heavenly Father to serve him always. This will help you to be worthy of your membership in the Church. Every time you partake of the Sacrament, you are renewing your promise—or covenant— which you made when you were baptized. You are to think of this very seriously while the Sacrament is being passed.

Let us look at our chart again. Baptism and the gift of the Holy Ghost are not the end of your journey at all. They have only brought you to the gate. You still have a long way to go on your journey through life. In order to reach your destination which is exaltation in the kingdom of God, you must follow the rest of the road signs very carefully. Some of these road-signs are: love, kindness, forgiveness, reverence, humility, obedience, the Word of Wisdom, tithing, honesty, thankfulness, prayer, and service. As I point to these road signs on our chart, please tell me about each one.

Your Heavenly Father loves you and will help

you always to do what is right. We, your parents, also love you dearly and are willing to do anything in the world for your happiness. We want so much to live together as a family in the hereafter—it is our earnest desire that each one of us in the family may follow the right path so that this will be possible.

We are most grateful that you are our child. You have been a blessing to us, and we know that as you continue along the gospel path you will bring us many more blessings and a great deal of joy. We are thrilled that you will soon be eight years old and able to be baptized and confirmed a member of the Church. We want you to know that we will do all we can to help you be a good member.

This is the journey of life—the way leading to eternal life. How glorious it will be some day to reach our destination: the kingdom of God where we may dwell together as a family with him forever and ever.

TELL ME ABOUT THE HOLY GHOST

Adapted from an article
in *The Instructor*, January
1964, by Charles R. Hobbs,
District Co-ordinator of
Southern Utah Seminaries

Suggested approach: Build a "bridge" to help a child understand deep gospel truths.

The Holy Ghost is a Personage of Spirit (Doctrine and Covenants 130:22), he is a mediator between God and man (John 14:26), he bestows gifts of the Spirit upon those who are worthy (Doctrine and Covenants 46:13-33), he assists one in being born again of the

Spirit (John 3:1-13), and through him comes a re-mission of sins upon conditions of repentance. (2 Nephi 31:17.) Yet would it not be fruitless to give such abstract explanations to a child?

Children can be given understanding of the Holy Ghost. Perhaps this is best illustrated and somewhat substantiated with the following metaphor:

Once there was a teacher who wanted to help a child whom he loved dearly. The student's name was Hope. This teacher lived on a large, beautiful plateau of knowledge. Hope dwelt on her own small plateau of limited knowledge which was separated from the larger one by a wide chasm of experience. The good teacher yearned to bring Hope into the adult world of understanding—to teach her about the Holy Ghost. This task seemed difficult. The gulf between them was wide.

After much thought, prayer, and preparation, the teacher found a way. He realized that this child her-self must walk the challenging gulf of experience. He was also aware of the dangers of false teachings and temptations which would confront Hope in this wide chasm.

The teacher knelt, then carefully extended him-self far below—even to the child's plateau of limited understanding. While descending, he became aware that but a short time earlier he, too, had lived in a child's world. It was indeed good to return to such a humble place again. From this lower plateau, the wise teacher grasped symbols and concepts familiar to his little protégée. With these he constructed a bridge across the chasm on which the child could easily walk. Now it was not necessary for little Hope to stare in bewilderment at the great plateau surfaced with its overwhelming words: mediator, bestowal of gifts, born again, manifestation, discernment, worthiness, and Personage of Spirit. Upon her bridge, which led eventually to these new concepts, she found her own vocabulary and simple concepts. On the bridge constructed by a wise teacher, Hope found many words and ideas which she could understand, such as,

> "The Holy Ghost makes me feel happy and warm inside when I keep Heavenly Father's commandments."

> "The Holy Ghost helps all those who do good and live the way Jesus wants them to."

> "When the Holy Ghost wants to prompt me, I must listen carefully; for he speaks very quietly in my mind."

> "The Holy Ghost looks like a man, but I cannot see him because he is a Spirit."

> "The Holy Ghost is sacred and holy because he is the third member of the Godhead."

> "The gift of the Holy Ghost will be given to me by men holding the Melchizedek Priesthood after I have been baptized."

> "The Holy Ghost gives spiritual gifts to those who have been baptized and live good lives."

> "The Holy Ghost bears witness unto men that Jesus really lives and that he is the Savior of the world. He reveals truth."

Hope's bridge was also constructed with comparisons. The questions of how the Holy Ghost can be with one person and not with another and of how the

Holy Ghost can be with many people at one time are easily understood when compared with the operation of a radio: To be baptized and live a good life is to turn on the radio. If the dial were never adjusted, the message would never be received. Any number of people can tune in to the same station and receive the same radio message. The Holy Ghost is capable of touching the lives of millions of people all at the same time. The bridge, structured with the above comparisons and with other simple analogies, made her progression toward the plateau of knowledge safer and surer.

* * *

It is important that our children understand the purpose and personality of the Holy Ghost, for it is the gift of the Holy Ghost that will lead them to exaltation and eternal life.

PRIESTHOOD POWER

Adapted from an analogy
by Mary Ellen Jolley

Suggested approach: an analogy to help young boys, as well as girls, understand and appreciate the power of the priesthood. The responsibilities and blessings of the priesthood could be discussed at length. A personal application in the life of the young person should be made. Some incidents relating the blessings the priesthood can bring to a family could be told. A father's testimony about his priesthood could be very effective.

Almost any family can receive electrical power from the power company. In order to get this, however, they must first have their house properly wired, and switch boxes and outlets must be installed. The wiring and the installations must pass inspection by a competent, authorized inspector.

The power is created by a great generator at the power plant. Lines are run from this generator through wires on poles. If a family wants to have this electricity brought into their home, connection will have to be made between the home and the power company's lines. The family, themselves, are not authorized to do so. An authorized representative from the power company will make the connection as soon as the wiring in the home has been approved and the family has made the proper request. After that, family members need only to turn on a switch to enjoy the advantages of electricity.

The priesthood of God is much like electricity. You can't see it, but you can feel its influence and power.

Almost any man can receive the priesthood. However, in order to do so he must meet certain conditions. First, he must personally live up to all the requirements. He must live so that he can pass an inspection in the form of an interview with the bishop.

The origin for priesthood power is with God himself. This power is given to the President of the Church who then gives it to others. No man can take this power upon himself. After he has been found worthy and has been interviewed, he is ordained by someone who has the authority to ordain or to make the connection. Now the man has the priesthood of God.

When there is electrical power in our home, we can enjoy as many conveniences as we want. We may choose only a few or we may have the added comforts and advantages of a number of conveniences. We can read by a small globe, a little bigger light, or by a large light. We can use every bit of electricity that is available, but we must keep our wiring in good condition, and we must pay the bill.

This is also true with the priesthood. A man may choose to utilize only a little power or he may have the many wonderful blessings of a great deal of power. If he is inactive, he will have only a small amount. If he is faithful in some things, he will have a larger amount of power. However, if he wants numerous blessings and a great deal of power, he must keep his own wiring in order by staying close to the leaders of the Church and to the Lord, and he must pay the bill by being active in the Church and faithful and devoted to his callings.

A young man who fails to be worthy of the priesthood, or a young girl who chooses to be married outside the temple, will have to live by a dim flashlight which runs on a weak battery. Because they aren't connected to the lines which lead to the generator, they will miss many blessings and opportunities.

When the priesthood is brought into the home through the worthiness of the husband, everyone in the family can enjoy a great amount of light and many blessings.

When a young man of the Church becomes twelve years of age, he is eligible, if he is worthy, to receive the priesthood. If this young man who has been ordained to the Aaronic Priesthood and who holds the office of a deacon, wants to live by a bright light, rather than a dim one, in due time he may become a teacher. Again, if he is fully worthy of his calling, he may later be ordained a priest and enjoy the full blessings of that office. If he continues to be faithful, he may, receive the Melchizedek Priesthood several years later and enjoy many more of the blessings our Father in heaven has prepared for us.

How do you want to live? By just a dim flashlight? By only a little light globe, or by all the light necessary to help you and your family some day enjoy a rich, beautiful life? It is all up to you. You must pay the bill.

LIFE IS LIKE A THREE ACT PLAY

PLAN OF SALVATION

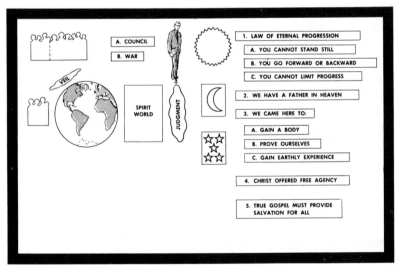

Flannelboard Demonstration

This lesson answers the questions: "Where did I come from?" "Why am I here?" and "Where am I going?" Through such a lesson a child can see how all phases of the gospel fit together to make a perfect whole. This lesson, according to the details which are presented, can help an eight-year-old child understand the gospel; it can challenge the thinking of an eighteen-year-old; or it can cause a mature person to gain a deeper understanding of the great plan of eternal life and the ways of our Father in heaven. The lesson as given here is written simply for children approximately eight to twelve years of age.

We have given this type of lesson many times before various Church groups, and invariably after each presentation someone comes up with tears in his eyes and says, "If I had understood those things thirty years ago, my life would have been different."

Often a mother has said, "I would give anything if my teenage son could hear that." Many other parents have asked to borrow our lesson outline and flannelboard figures that they might present this subject to their children many times until they know it well, so that their lives might be different!

With these thoughts in mind, we have written this lesson so that you may use it to help your children better understand the purpose of life.

Life is like a three-act play. Here on earth we find ourselves in the second act. We can play our part more intelligently if we know something of what took place in the first act and what we can expect in the third act. Because of the restoration of the gospel, we have knowledge of our pre-earth life and life hereafter. The gospel also helps us to find our part here so that the third act can be a glorious one.

Before we came to this earth, we were spirits and dwelled in the presence of our Father in heaven.

Just as people here on earth are different in personality and abilities, we spirits had individual traits and characteristics. Some spirits were more diligent than others and took advantage of their time to develop themselves and make improvement, while others were lazy and failed to go forward. Through a natural process, some intelligences rose above others; they made more progress. Can you tell me what the word "progress" means? Yes, it means to go forward, to advance, to improve or become better.

Is it possible to stand still? No, there is a law of eternal progression which means that one must always progress. You cannot stand still. You go either forward or backward.

Do you think there is a limit to the progress you can make? No, of course not. When a child reaches five years of age, he knows how to walk and talk. When he turns six, he doesn't have to learn how to walk and talk all over again, but he can go on learning new things such as how to read or write or how to play simple tunes on the piano. Throughout our lives we can go on learning and progressing. We can continue to make progress throughout eternity—forever and ever. That is one of the most beautiful things about the gospel and one thing which helps me to know that it is true and certainly the plan of our Father in heaven.

The purpose of this progression is to become like our Father in heaven. He is perfect and some day, we, too, are to become perfect. We know that this is possible because throughout our lives we must continue to make progress, otherwise we will go backward.

Our Father in heaven is a Spirit *plus* a body. His Spirit is perfect, and his body has been glorified so that it can live forever. In order for us to become as he is, we, too, must develop our spirits to perfection. Also,

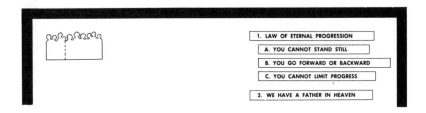

| 1. LAW OF ETERNAL PROGRESSION |
| A. YOU CANNOT STAND STILL |
| B. YOU GO FORWARD OR BACKWARD |
| C. YOU CANNOT LIMIT PROGRESS |
| 2. WE HAVE A FATHER IN HEAVEN |

we had to gain a body (remember, in the pre-existence we were only spirits) which could someday become resurrected and glorified.

In order to become like our Father in heaven and return to him some day, it is necessary that we prove our worthiness—to show him that we are worthy of living with him in heaven.

If I put you to bed and tell you that you must stay there, then sit by your side ready to spank you if you get out, I'm sure that you would stay in bed. But if I tell you that you must stay there and then I leave the room, you are free to do as you wish. You know the rule or the law. You know that if you don't go to sleep, you'll be too tired the next morning to do well in school. Still you are free to do what you want. This is the real test. Only after I leave can you prove your obedience and worthiness to me.

Also, in order to become perfect as our Father in heaven is, we must have earthly experiences. We, as your parents, can share many of our experiences with you and help you to learn from us, but there are many lessons you must learn for yourself; for instance, I could sit here and tell you all about how I learned to drive a car and explain to you the steps involved in driving a car. But until you actually try this yourself, you don't really know how to drive. You must experience it to know.

Our Father in heaven called a meeting or council while we were in the pre-existence. You and I—everyone—were present. The Father presented a plan whereby we could do these three important things: (1) gain a body, (2) prove ourselves, and (3) gain earthly experience. He had organized an earth, and we were to come to this earth to do these things and continue our progression.

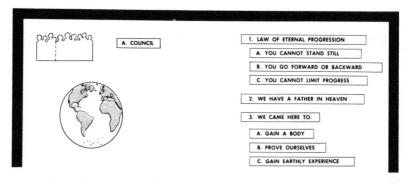

Our Father in heaven explained how man would become mortal and eventually die. He told of the need for a Redeemer or Savior to save us from death and prepare the way so that we could someday become resurrected and have glorified bodies and return to him to live forever.

Two spirits offered to save mankind. One, who was named Lucifer, said he would come to earth and make or force everyone to be good. Instead of letting man be free and choose for himself, he would force him to be obedient. He said that he would save everyone and then wanted to have all the honor and glory for doing so.

The other spirit who volunteered to be the Savior was Jesus Christ. He accepted the plan of the Father and said he would show the people through example and teachings the right way to live, but that he would let them be free to choose as they desired. He said, "Father, thy will be done and the glory be thine forever."

Jesus Christ was chosen to be the Savior of the world. Lucifer rebelled and caused a war in heaven. He was defeated and with one third of the hosts (or spirits) of heaven, he was cast out and become Satan or the devil.

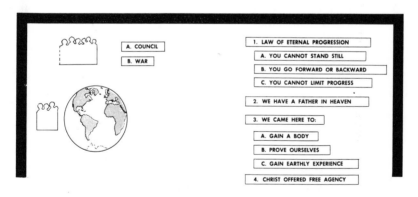

Jesus Christ, the Savior of the world, has protected for us our great gift of free agency. He has shown us the way, but we are free to do as we choose. This way we can truly prove our worthiness. There is no point in taking a test if someone is telling us the answers!

In order to have free agency, a veil has been drawn across our minds. We cannot remember the things which took place or that which we did in the pre-existence. If the little child who was supposed to stay in bed knew that his mother was out in the hall looking through the key hole, prepared to punish him if he got out, he would naturally stay in bed. We must live by faith.

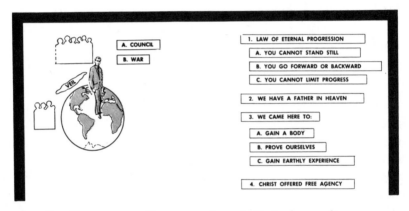

In its proper time, each spirit is born here upon the earth. You, (*name of child*), came down to earth and were given the great blessing of a body. Now you are able further to prove yourself to your Father in heaven and gain the experiences necessary for your exaltation or eternal life.

Our Father in heaven expects four things of you. First, you are to have faith. Do you know what faith is? Yes, it means to believe. You are to learn about our wonderful world and gain a strong belief in God, the Creator of the world. You are also to learn about Jesus Christ and his life and death and have faith that because of him you, too, will someday be resurrected.

As you learn about Heavenly Father and Jesus Christ and the gospel, you will want to try harder and harder to do all that they say. You will want to become a better person each day. Whenever you try to be better or improve in some way, you are repenting. The second thing which our Father in heaven wants you to do is to repent. Remember, when we had our lesson on baptism, we talked a great deal about repentance. When we repent, we make progress and become more perfect.

After you have faith and are worthy through repentance, the third thing our Father in heaven requires of you is to become baptized. Through baptism you become a member of the kingdom of God.

Then when you are confirmed a member of the Church, our Father in heaven gives you a special blessing or gift to help you be a good member of the Church. What is this special gift? Yes, it is the gift of the Holy Ghost. The fourth thing our Father in heaven requires of us is that we live righteously and are faithful every day of our lives. The Holy Ghost helps us to know the difference between right and wrong and helps us to live the commandments of our Father in heaven.

It is really a blessing to have the gift of the Holy Ghost, because ever since Lucifer or the devil and his followers were cast out of heaven, the only way they've been able to make progress is to try to win more souls to their side. So the devil and his helpers will work very, very hard to tempt you and try to lead you away from the things which are right. They have been tempting people for a long, long time and know just where we are weak and how they can lead us down the wrong path. But the devil can have no power over you whatsoever if you stay close to the teachings of

the Lord and listen carefully to the promptings of the
Holy Ghost.

As you learned when we talked about baptism,
baptism is just the gate to our Heavenly Father's kingdom. There is still a long path which you must follow
to reach the presence of our Father in heaven. In order
to keep on the right path, you must learn all you can
about the gospel and the commandments of our Father
in heaven. You are always to attend Sunday School,
Sacrament meeting, and Primary regularly. When you
are older, it will also be your privilege to go to priesthood meeting (in the case of a boy), MIA, and seminary. You are to love and serve others and be honest
and fair in all that you do. You are to pay your tithing
and keep the Word of Wisdom. When worthy boys
become twelve years of age, they are given the priesthood, and they are to understand and honor it and use
it for the blessing of others in the Church and their
own families some day.

If boys honor the priesthood and live good, clean
lives, when they are about nineteen, they will have the
privilege of being called on missions. Then they can
go out in the world and tell other people about the
wonderful things our Father in heaven has planned
for us. Preaching the gospel and sharing one's testimony with others is one of the choicest blessings anyone could ever have.

Then as you continue along the right path, you
will someday meet a wonderful person whom you will
want to have as your companion. You will go to the
temple of the Lord and be married so that you may
be married in heaven, too, and live together and love
each other forever. Later you will become parents and
raise a fine family. If you live the gospel and teach

your children to do so, you may be together as a family in heaven. To have your loved ones with you for all eternity is the greatest blessing of all.

Then some day when your work here on earth has been completed, our Father in heaven will call you home. Your body will be laid to rest in the ground and your spirit will go on to the spirit world. After we die, we don't go directly to the third act. Between this life and our life in heaven there is an intermission. We call it the spirit world.

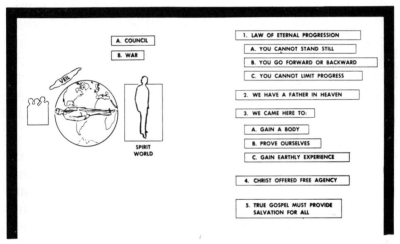

There is a very special work to be done in this spirit world. You know, we are all children of our Father in heaven and he loves each one of us very much. He wants to help us in every way so that we can return to him and live with him throughout all eternity. In order to go to the part of heaven where our Father in heaven lives, you have to know and live the gospel and be baptized.

Even though the Church has thousands of mis-

sionaries out preaching the gospel to people all over
the world, there are still many, many people who live
and die without ever hearing about the gospel or having the chance to accept and live it. Do you think it
would be fair if they couldn't return to Heavenly
Father just because they never had the opportunity to
hear about the gospel? Of course not. Our Heavenly
Father treats all of his children exactly alike. Therefore everyone who ever lived will have the chance to
hear the gospel and accept it or reject it, according to
his own free agency. The purpose of the spirit world
is to provide the opportunity for everyone to hear
about the gospel. Those of us who know and understand the gospel can serve as missionaries and preach
to those who have not. Then those spirits can have
faith and they can repent. Also, they must become
baptized, but they cannot be baptized in the spirit
world. That is something which must be done here
on earth. But our Father in heaven, in his great wisdom, has a solution to this problem. We, who are still
on earth can go to one of the temples and be baptized
for a dead person. Then this person, who is now in the
spirit world, can either accept or reject this baptism.
If he accepts the baptism, then he can continue his
progression and is worthy of our Father in heaven's
choice blessings.

Then after your work in the spirit world has been
accomplished, you will be resurrected, which means
that your spirit will once again be clothed by your
body. This time, however, your body will be a glorified
one which will never die again but which will live
forever.

After this, you will go to the judgment bar where
all of your actions will be reviewed and your worthiness will be determined. The veil which has been placed

over your mind will be removed, and you will be able to remember all that you did in the pre-existence as well as what your actions on earth were. Then you will know whether or not you are worthy of our Father in heaven's presence.

Everyone will be judged according to his works, and there will be a place for everyone. We are told by our prophets that there are three degrees of glory in heaven. The lowest degree is the telestial world. This is the place where people will go who have not kept either the laws of the Lord or the laws of the land. These are the murderers, thieves, and wicked people of the world.

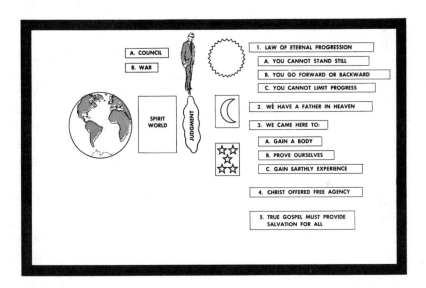

The second degree of glory is the terrestrial world. Here people will go who have kept the laws of the land, but who have not kept all of the laws of God. These people are good people, but they either were not baptized or they failed to follow the right path after their baptism. These people, as well as those in the telestial world, will not enjoy the presence of our Father in heaven and they will not have the blessing of eternal marriage or family life.

The highest degree of glory is the celestial kingdom. This is the kingdom of our Father in heaven; this is where he dwells along with the righteous, valiant people. People who are worthy of this kingdom are the ones who have kept all the laws of the land and all the laws of God. They are faithful, wonderful people who were baptized and who kept the commandments of the Lord all their lives. In the celestial kingdom they will enjoy all the glorious blessings of our Father in heaven. They will dwell in his presence and will have the precious blessing of eternal marriage and family life.

(*Name of child*), you are on the path which leads to the celestial kingdom. You have been baptized (or soon will be, as the case may be) and have the gift of the Holy Ghost to guide and direct you. If you listen to the promptings of this Spirit, follow the advice of your parents and the counsel of the prophet of the Lord, and pray earnestly to your Father in heaven, you will be able to keep on this path and be worthy of some day being a member of the kingdom of God: the celestial kingdom.

More than anything else in the world, Mother and Daddy want you to be good and faithful and always do what is right so we can be together and enjoy glorious blessings forever and ever. It is our constant prayer that we, you and I and everyone in our family, will live so that someday when we meet our Father in heaven, he will welcome us into his kingdom by saying, "Well done, thou good and faithful servant. Enter thou into the joy of the Lord." (See Matt. 25:21.)

How to Do Less for Your Children So You Can Do More with Them

How to Do Less for Your Children
So You Can Do More with Them

In order to have the time and energy to apply the principles and ideas contained in this book, the children will have to share in the responsibility and work of running the home. A mother cannot be efficient or hard-working enough to keep up the housework and do meaningful things with children if the children are thoughtless, careless and uncooperative. But when children work with the mother, rather than against her, the housework isn't much of a problem and there is time for growth and development and special family experiences. Great families work together and then play and grow together!

Furthermore, children need the training which comes through having responsibility and learning to work. An ideal home is like an apprentice shop where children learn skills, habits, responsibility, dependability and self-discipline. It is especially important that children are trained to develop self-discipline. It's not difficult to learn to make a bed; the challenge lies in making it *every* day! And children who gain mastery over little things (such as making beds) will have power over greater things.

This sounds great in theory; the question is: *how* can a mother help her children to help her without declaring "war" on them?

Let's discuss this under seven categories:

1. GIVE CHILDREN AN INCENTIVE

Everyone works better with incentives. (Like the woman who says she has no trouble at all getting out of bed in the morning if she thinks: "My mother-in-law might visit today!")

A wise parent will motivate children by providing incentives for them until they're mature enough to establish their own. Don't be concerned if you have to use a great variety of incentives; beneath them children are building habits and values so they'll one day be self-motivated and self-disciplined persons.

Some incentives which appeal to children are:

> When the dishes are done, we'll bake cookies;
> When the weeds are pulled, we'll go swimming;
> When the toys are picked up and you're ready for bed, I'll read you a story;
> When your homework is finished, you may play ball;
> After you've done your practicing, you may go shopping with me.

Be sure that you don't confuse incentives with bribes. It is better to say, "When the weeds are pulled, we'll go swimming," than "If you pull the weeds, I'll take you swimming."

2. MAKE WORK FUN FOR CHILDREN

Help your children realize that work is a blessing, not a burden. A mother's attitude toward work is reflected by her children. In other words, if she has a positive outlook toward her responsibilities and role in life, her children are very likely to share the same positive outlook. Remember, attitudes are "caught," not "taught."

Games help children develop a healthy attitude toward work. (And they help motivate them, too.) Some suggested games are:

Let a child wear a little hand puppet (made from a

sock or paper bag) as he picks up his toys. Allow him to tell the puppet what to do, which is a pleasant change from mother telling him what to do.

At bedtime one father plays army with his two little boys. He assigns them a rank, has them march and drill and before the children realize what's happened, they've picked up their playthings, put on their night clothes and have paraded off to bed. (The amazing thing about this "fun approach" is that it actually requires less time than is involved in the usual going-to-bed struggle.)

"Titles" make work fun, such as: Dust Deputy, Kitchen Katie, Bathroom Butch, Parlor Polly . . .

For making fun work out of kitchen chores, let children draw cards which read:

Jolly Jump-Up	serves during meal and answers telephone or doorbell
Snappy Scraper	scrapes and stacks dishes
Wow-of-a-Washer	loads dishwasher or washes dishes
Pert Polisher	wipes off tables, chairs, counter tops, range and refrigerator

A game that never seems to grow old is "Twenty-Pick-Up." Perhaps a room, such as the playroom, is cluttered with toys, books or papers. Call the children together and ask them each to pick up and put away twenty things, or whatever number of items appears necessary. Watch the clutter disappear like magic because through such a game the children see both the beginning and the end of their chore, which is very encouraging, and they don't have to worry whether or not others in the family are doing their part. Try "Twenty-Pick-Up" next time your home or yard is cluttered or when there are weeds to pull or someone drops the can of crayons.

3. MAKE WORK EASY FOR CHILDREN

Don't just tell them to do a job. *Show them how*!
Help a young child, who is very eager at ages two and
three, make his bed every morning for several years.
Then by the time he is physically able to handle the
task (by about five-years-of-age) making his bed has
become a habit.

Take the time to really train a child to clean the
bathroom, work in the kichen, bake cookies, sweep a
floor, or care for the yard.

Install for your children low shelves and low
clothes rods so minimum effort is required to put
things away and hang things away.

A sample table place setting made from colored
construction paper (see illustration) provides a handy

pattern for children as they set the table. And they're
more willing workers when their chances for doing a
job successfully are insured.

Drawstring bags, tin cans with plastic tops or
sturdy boxes make good containers for toys that have
many parts or pieces and make caring for toys fun and
easy.

Performing a task is easy, if you know how. Remember, a home should be like an apprentice shop. Children love it that way because *skills bring thrills*!

4. BE CONSISTENT IN REQUIRING CHILDREN'S HELP

Invariably little Billy would come to the dinner table with dirty hands and face and would, of course, be sent away to wash. One day mother was exasperated and said, "Goodness, Billy, why do you always come to the table without washing? You know I'll send you away and make you do it."

"Well, you see," explained Billy, "once you forgot."

Even though the type of job may vary from day to day, children should be used to fulfilling some kind of responsibility every day. If you as a mother had children help yesterday but don't require help today, then should you ask for help tomorrow, it's likely they'll try to argue and talk you out of it because they feel you aren't sure of yourself.

Decide what you expect and then stick to it. Your children will soon realize your mind is made up and the arguing will cease. They will accept their assignments as a matter of routine.

Exceptions could be holidays, birthdays, when a child is ill or when some special activity or opportunity presents itself. When a legitimate exception is made, it is not a sign of inconsistency but rather of fairness and good sense. Children will respond eagerly to this and will be willing to fall back into the pattern when things return to normal.

Few, if any, people are completely consistent, however. So when you forget or slip a little, be big and wise enough to admit it to your child. Apologize by saying, "I'm sorry. I failed to do as I should. I'll try

harder." Everyone makes mistakes; let your child see
you handle yours in a mature way.

5. ORGANIZE CHILDREN'S WORK FOR THEM

When work is organized and systematized, it can
be accomplished in half the time. Even a young child
appreciates this!

Chore lists are one good way to organize work.
They eliminate interrupting, nagging, reminding, and
forgetting (on part of both mother and child). Besides,
lists are actually therapeutic in their effect; it's exciting to tackle them and rewarding to cross items off!

Lists can be posted on the bulletin board, on the
wall or side of the refrigerator, or under each child's
breakfast plate. Children also enjoy a "job jar" where
each child draws a given number of slips of paper with
chores listed on them.

Deadlines help organize work for children. A
family policy could be that no one is served breakfast
until he is washed and dressed. (It takes a child about
two minutes to dress before breakfast and about two
hours afterwards!) The policy could further state that
no child may leave for school or play until his basic
morning chores are done, such as making the bed and
putting the bedroom in order, dusting the furniture,
helping in the kitchen or carrying out the garbage.
Evening projects may not be started until the child has
done his homework, completed his musical practicing
and so forth.

6. DISCIPLINE CHILDREN EFFECTIVELY
WHEN NECESSARY

There are times in every home when making work
exciting, fun, easy, fair and organized doesn't get it
done. Then effective discipline is necessary. Wise

parents realize that discipline should be a *learning* experience, not just a punishment. Through punishment a parent controls a child's actions, but that isn't enough. Through good discipline a parent can teach a child to control his own actions. (Joseph Smith said he taught his people correct principles and they governed themselves. Parents should do the same thing for their children.)

The most effective way to discipline a child is through application of the law of cause and effect. In other words, if a parents lets a child feel the *effect* or *consequences* of his own negative actions, he'll have a true learning experience and be headed toward self-control.

Life itself—consequences—really teaches children vital lessons quickly. The use of consequences eliminates much scolding, punishing and nagging on the part of parents. As a result, rebellion and resentment are not built up within the child. A child has a keen sense of fair play. A consequence is fair—it is exactly what he deserves—so he takes his medicine and seldom needs a second dose.

There are two types of consequences:

Natural—where a parent stands back and lets life itself teach a child.

Example: A child doesn't come for dinner when he's called so he misses dinner and doesn't eat anything until breakfast.

Logical—where there isn't a natural consequence or else it is dangerous, so a logical consequence is structured by the parents.

Example: A child starts to play in the street so he is removed to the house. (If he cannot handle his freedom to play outside without going into the street, then he loses his freedom.)

Examples of consequences as they apply to teaching children to share in the responsibility of the home:

If a child's dirty clothes are not put in the hamper or clothes chute, then the clothes cannot be washed by the mother. He either wears dirty clothes or washes them himself.

If a child doesn't put away his toys, they may be placed on the "unwanted toy shelf" until he has missed them sufficiently to take better care of them.

If older children (or mothers or fathers!) leave articles of clothing or other belongings littered around, these articles may be placed in a "mad bag." (The mad bag is just a large grocery bag in which neglected items are kept until redeemed by the owner with a nickel or dime. The money, of course, goes to the person who had to pick up the items to compensate him or her for the "undue maid service" he or she had to render. Or if the owner of the neglected items is low on cash, he may redeem his things by performing some special service for the person who had to pick up after him. (Once in a while it might be necessary to declare a "mad bag emptying day" in which no one leaves the house until all his articles have been redeemed.

When children balk about doing the dishes, the consequence is that anyone who is "too tired" or "too busy" to do the dishes, is also "too tired" or "too busy" to receive any phone calls or watch television that evening and must spend his time resting in his room with lights out and music off. Being aroused from bed for a trip to the garage may be required for the boy who leaves his bike out or forgets to set out the garbage cans.

If a child carelessly loses or breaks something, he must replace the item with his money, or at least make a substantial contribution, according to his age, toward its replacement.

If a child leaves without making his bed and putting his room in order, he may be called home from school or play to do such. (What's a lesson in arithmetic if he cannot handle basic responsibility?)

If parents return home after an evening out and find the house in shambles when the children had been instructed to tidy up, being awakened at a late hour to do so helps children to forevermore follow instructions.

A family was driving in the car with the children fussing and arguing about sitting by the windows. So the father turned the car around, took the family home and had each child sit by a window of the house for an hour!

Even though this approach to discipline is a drastic one, it is not harsh or cruel. *And it is effective.* It is a Christ-like method based on His law. The Lord himself has said: "There is a law, irrevocably decreed in heaven before the foundations of this world, upon which all blessings are predicated—And when we obtain any blessing from God, it is by obedience to that law upon which it is predicated." (Doctrine & Covenants 130:20-21)

Because it's difficult to think creatively during a moment of crisis, a wise parent will plan in advance what consequence could be used to fit a certain situation. In other words, it would be well to make a list of typical family problems and then take time to think through what consequences could apply. Then when the next problem arises, the parent, instead of desperately resorting to yelling, threatening or punishing, would be prepared to discipline the child effectively. Then a true learning experience would be had by the child.

This method also helps a parent avoid a power clash with a child. It is impossible and wrong to force a child. And if a parent attempts to do this, he'll likely reduce himself to a desperate, yelling ogre, accomplishing nothing but undermining both his and his child's self-respect. *Even though a parent cannot force a child, the parent can determine what he as a parent is going to do and in that way he can control the child.* For example: a parent cannot, without being a brute, make a child do a certain task. But he can forbid the child to leave the house until the task is done. For every five minutes the child stalls, the parent can "ground" the child an hour.

Another example: If children are fighting over which television channel to watch, instead of trying to solve the problem for them and thereby joining the fight, a parent need merely turn off the set and say: "When you have solved your problem, you may turn the TV back on." Within seconds the children will have made the decision and will be happily and quietly watching TV.

Another one: If a child's crying annoys you, don't try to stop it. Merely leave the room or take the child to his own room. He'll soon stop crying because it's no fun to cry without an audience!

When a child is made to feel responsible for his own self and affairs, he gains in maturity and the parent is free from annoying problems which he shouldn't try to solve, anyway. For instance, a little girl came running home to Mother with the complaint that children were throwing sticks at her. The mother said, "Well, come in the house if it bothers you." The child quickly responded, "Oh, it doesn't," and happily ran back to play.

For further information about these and other extremely helpful ideas on child guidance, refer to *Children the Challenge* by Rudolf Dreikurs, M.D., published by Duell, Sloan & Pearce. Dr. Hugh G. Allred of Brigham Young University, in his book, *A Mission for Mother* effectively treats this same theory from an L.D.S. viewpoint.

A helpful book about understanding children and communicating with them is *Between Parent and Child* by Haim G. Ginott.

7. LET CHILDREN FEEL APPRECIATION FOR THEIR EFFORTS

Children will do almost anything for a parent's smile, a nod of approval or a sincere word of thanks.

Besides expressing appreciation in the usual manner, try some unusual ways, such as:

Write notes and place them under your children's pillows, tucked in their lunch pails, placed inside balloons which are then blown up and secured to the ceilings of their rooms. Write them special birthday love letters. Place little jingles such as this one on their dressers:

> I'm really not a poet,
> But in some way I must show it;
> I think it's really great
> The way you keep your room so straight!

If for some reason your children have been negligent about doing their chores or you haven't trained and taught them to work as you should or they are just reaching the age to be really helpful and you feel *now* is the time to act, *be careful*! Proceed carefully and gradually. Remember, two jobs done well are worth six on the list.

In many homes children are not paid for doing any of their routine chores. These chores are part of living together as a family just like the meals and fun times. If you pay your child to make his bed, for instance, and then the day comes when he has a job and earns money, he'll see no reason why he should continue making his bed. On the other hand, there could be a few paid jobs to supplement the children's allowance and to teach them the satisfaction of earning money. But these are not routine, basic chores. These paid jobs are chores for which you might hire someone to perform and hire instead your own child. For example, you might hire your older girls to baby sit the younger children. You might hire your teenage boy to paint the house. If the girls don't want to baby sit or if your son doesn't want to paint the house, you could hire someone else without losing face. It's strictly a business proposition. Make certain you establish the distinction between a required job and a hired job.

Just a word about the various ages and stages of children and how they relate to their chores. Toddlers and very young children are eager to help, especially if the job involves water or knives! It's wise whenever possible to capitalize on their willingness. It is inconsistent to refuse to let a child help set the table when he's two and then, when he's six, demand that he do it. At least the two-year-old can place napkins and silverware. Unless the task is either dangerous or destructive, you should let a child have the fun and growth which comes from trying.

Then the novelty of helping—unless the task is especially challenging—begins to wane as the child approaches three. A pre-schooler must be motivated before he will work. Lots of the suggestions already mentioned in this chapter appeal to children of this age group.

Children from age six to eleven usually give the best help around the house. So this is the age to train them to be really effective in their responsibilities and to make certain that proper work habits and traits are being formed.

As you may well know, many older children and teenagers are so very busy with studies, part-time jobs and social activities that they don't have as much time to help around the house as they did when they were younger. They are out doing the things you've prepared them for! Even so, if a teenager has had early and consistent training in doing chores so that he has good work habits, and if the home is organized so that the time spent on chores is at a minimum, there are a number of things he can do to help. Even the busiest teenager should keep his own room and clothing in order and should not make work for someone else through his sloppiness and inconsideration.

Times have changed and there generally is not enough outside work or heavy chores to provide a boy with enough responsibility. So it's all right for him to do any type of work around the home. However, the heavier jobs should be his first responsibility. But good work habits, dependability, careful and wise use of time, and thoroughness can be learned whether through milking cows or doing the dishes.

As a boy carries out household chores, his mother may remind him occasionally that this is all helping him to someday be a good business executive or construction engineer or to succeed in any profession. Also, this will help him to be a more considerate, understanding and thoughtful husband. Just as long as the boy has a good father image—his father is the head of the house and is worthy of everyone's respect—and can see his mother as a gracious, lovely homemaker, household chores can only make him grow to be a better man.

Teaching children to work and putting up with all their messes and inadequacies is a real challenge. It would be lots easier to shoo your children out of the house, lock the door, and do it all yourself. But that's not what mothers are for. When someone said that mothers are supposed to sacrifice for their children, surely they had this in mind.

It takes years of teaching, training, showing, patience, diligence, understanding, and encouragement, along with lots and lots of follow-up, to really prepare a child to be a good worker who can make a contribution in life. But when he finally learns, his accomplishments and successes will make all your efforts more than worthwhile. Dorothy Canfield Fisher said: "A mother is not a person to lean on. Rather she is a person to make leaning unnecessary."

Elder Richard L. Evans put all this philosophy in a nutshell when he said: "A few headaches now will save you from heartaches later on."

SUGGESTED CHORES FOR CHILDREN

Three-Year-Old Child

Daily

Before Breakfast

    dress
    put pajamas away
    brush teeth
    wash face
    comb hair
    make bed (with help)
    tidy up bedroom

Before Play

    help dust bedroom
      furniture

After Lunch

    help clear lunch table

Before Story Hour and
    Bedtime

    pick up toys, etc.
    prepare for bed

Weekly

Before Play

    empty waste baskets
    tend garden (in sea-
      son)
    clean up assigned
      area of yard

When Necessary

    help clean closet
      and drawers

Five-Year-Old Child

Daily

Before Breakfast

    dress
    put pajamas away
    brush teeth
    wash face
    comb hair
    make bed (with help
      occasionally)
    tidy up room

Weekly

Before Play

    empty waste baskets
    clean tile walls in
      bathroom
    tend garden (in sea-
      son)
    clean up assigned
      area of yard

When Necessary

    help clean drawers
      and closet

Six-Year-Old Child

Daily	Weekly	When Necessary
Before Breakfast	return empty garbage cans to garage	help clean closet and drawers
dress	tend garden (in season)	
put pajamas away	clean up assigned area of yard	
brush teeth	clean interior of car	
wash face	sweep porches and walks	
comb hair	clean kitchen table and chair legs	
make bed		
tidy up room		
feed pets		
Before School/Play		
dust bedroom furniture		
set breakfast table		
take out kitchen garbage		
After Lunch		
return to school or quiet time for reading, crafts		
After Dinner		
clear table and help clean up kitchen		
Before Story Hour and Bedtime		
pick up toys, etc.		
prepare for bed		
read and study		

Eight-Year-Old Child

same basic chores as for six-year-old with the addition of
helping clean bathroom, dusting furniture throughout the house,
ironing simple articles and helping fold away freshly
laundered clothing

Older Children

change linen on bed
clean entire bathroom
clean kitchen well after meals
assume full responsibility for the care of one room, eventually entire house
vacuum carpeting, ledges, ridges, upholstery, etc.
iron
cook and bake
plan meals
do marketing
sew and mend (girls)
repair jobs (boys)
practice musical instruments
scrub and wax floors
assume full responsibility of managing home for a week or so
take complete charge of personal grooming
assume full responsibility of personal clothing (shopping, care, etc.)
defrost refrigerator or freezer
clean range
help with heavy spring cleaning
paint
refinish furniture
wash and wax car
yard work

INDEX

INDEX

W

Watkins, Arthur V., xvi
What to say—How to say it, 179-80
Whitman, Walt, 97
Work, 15, 224-28, 233-39
Worsley, Klea, 11
Worthiness, 196-98

Y

Young, Brigham, 45, 51
Your Child's Self-Esteem, 11-12

Z

ZCMIRROR, 22